PRAISE FOR
REAL CHRISTIAN

As Todd explains, *real is something you ca*[...] brought us from darkness to light, it wil[...] able ways in our hearts. In an age of ext[...] books on spirituality, this book goes right to the heart of true Christianity. I'm excited to recommend this well-written, biblical, and gospel-driven book to new and experienced Christians seeking not only to recognize the evidences of the new birth within them but also to understand what separates the Christian gospel from every other message in the world.

J.D. Greear, pastor of The Summit Church
and author of *Stop Asking Jesus into Your Heart*

Taking his cues from Jonathan Edwards's *Religious Affections* and remaining rigorously biblical on every point, Todd Wilson has given us a powerful (and at times painful) antidote to inauthentic Christianity. Many who think they are Christians will not recognize themselves in this book (and will, I hope, be brought to repentance), while those who actually are will be challenged to an even more passionate pursuit of that holiness apart from which no one will see God. Highly recommended!

Sam Storms, pastor of Bridgeway Church in Oklahoma City

What do you find on apple trees? Apples. *What do you find on orange trees?* Oranges. *So what do you find on Christians?* Christians bear fruit too. And our assurance of salvation is this—Jesus said, "You will recognize them by their fruits" (Matthew 7:16). Jesus also said, "The one who endures to the end will be saved" (Matthew 24:13). These are the marks of a real Christian. Todd Wilson gets it right in this great resource. He's the real deal, and so is this book.

James MacDonald, senior pastor of Harvest Bible Chapel,
author of *Vertical Church*, and founder of
Act Like Men conferences; jamesmacdonald.org

This is a book about reality—real Christians who have been delivered out of darkness into the divine light that is Jesus Christ. The marks of a Christian profiled in this book are a call to discipleship. They are also a call to transformation—piercing, enduring, and leading at the end of the day to joy, real joy. A great primer on the spiritual life.

Timothy George, founding dean of Beeson Divinity School of Samford University and general editor of the *Reformation Commentary on Scripture*

I loved this book! I was alternately encouraged and challenged as Todd Wilson guided me through the key marks of real Christianity as revealed in our lives. His careful teaching about humility stands out for how it clarifies our mistaken notions. Now I'm praying that God will give me the opportunity to walk through this delightfully biblical and compelling book with a new Christian or with someone considering the claims of Jesus.

Collin Hansen, editorial director of The Gospel Coalition and coauthor of *A God-Sized Vision*

Todd Wilson is a genuine pastor-scholar. With a heart for people and a mind for God—and a mind for people and a heart for God—Wilson unleashes a challenging message for a church drunk on safety and security. *Real Christian* is a gem. Written with sparkling clarity and rich conviction, this book will burn off the blinding fog of spirituality that hinders genuine faith. The American church desperately needs this book!

Preston M. Sprinkle, PhD, director of Eternity Bible College's Boise extension site and author of *Fight* **and** *Paul and Judaism Revisited*

Todd Wilson's *Real Christian* is exactly the book we need at this moment. It shows us that real faith in Christ truly changes us. It isn't enough to say you're real; real Christianity has effects in our lives that are visible, and Todd shows what those are. What we see is radically biblical, and yet not what we often think—which is exactly why this book is so important. Todd writes with a humility and clarity that is convicting and yet hopeful. Instead of throwing us back on ourselves, he points us to Christ in a way that few books today do. This book can help the church recover its authentic witness. I cannot recommend it highly enough.

Matt Perman, author of *What's Best Next: How the Gospel Transforms the Way You Get Things Done*

Todd Wilson's new book shows that real Christian discipleship is about deliberately cultivating Christlikeness. He shows what it is that separates followers from fans. Wilson encourages readers to leave behind a mediocre faith and shows them how to get serious about following Jesus. A great guide on how to grow into Christian virtue, foster spiritual fruitfulness, and gain godly character.

Michael F. Bird (PhD, University of Queensland), lecturer in theology at Ridley Melbourne Mission and Ministry College in Australia

Jonathan Edwards spent his life impressing real, spiritual truths on the hearts and minds of others, helping them sense the reality of things revealed in the Bible. Here, Todd Wilson renders these things real to the rest of us. Using Edwards's best-known book, *A Treatise Concerning Religious Affections*, Wilson shows us what it means to be a genuine child of God. In crisp, clear, compelling prose, he helps us see what God has done for us in Jesus and the cross, and what he is able to do in people he transforms by his Spirit and suffuses with his love. Please take this book and read it. God wants to make *you* real.

Douglas A. Sweeney, Trinity Evangelical Divinity School

Professing faith doesn't always equate to possessing faith. According to Todd Wilson, you can fake being a Christian by merely learning doctrine or modifying your behavior, but a real Christian is someone with a transformed heart who produces the marks of authentic faith — humility, meekness, contrition, wholeness, hunger, and perfected love. Grounded in Scripture and guided by heroes of the faith, Wilson offers a prophetic call to a world longing for authenticity but peddling with superficiality.

Jeremy Treat, pastor at Reality LA in Hollywood,
adjunct professor at Biola University,
and author of _The Crucified King_

Read this book. Soak in it. Savor each word like you would each bite of a fine meal. _Real Christian_ is strong, convicting, and inspiring. It's unvarnished but filled with light. It's powerful yet approachable. After every chapter I wanted more. More of Christ. More of what I need for my journey with Christ. More of the power that should accompany an authentic walk with Christ. More of being marked by the signs of following Jesus. It's practical without being just another how-to book. It's profound and fresh at the same time. Yes—a thousand times, yes.

Dan Wolgemuth, president and CEO of Youth for Christ/USA

Real Christian is a journey down the "ancient paths . . . where the good way is." But this isn't a "been there, done that" sort of read! Todd Wilson's lively style and challenging applications helped me see both God's truth and my own heart in fresh and redemptive ways. The chapter on meekness is alone worth the price of the book, making these pages ones worth traveling more than once!

Randall J. Gruendyke, campus pastor at Taylor University

True conversion is an act of grace, through Jesus Christ, by the power of the Holy Spirit. Period. But true conversion has necessary evidences that accompany it. Justification by faith alone is a reality that can be seen and experienced, and naming this reality serves to make much of this cardinal doctrine. Todd Wilson has captured the beauty of gospel transformation in this practical work by uncovering the nature and evidences of real Christianity—one that gifts us with actual godliness.

Jay Thomas, lead pastor of Chapel Hill Bible Church

REAL
CHRISTIAN

REAL
CHRISTIAN

BEARING THE MARKS OF AUTHENTIC FAITH

TODD WILSON

 ZONDERVAN®

ZONDERVAN

Real Christian
Copyright © 2014 by Todd A. Wilson

This title is also available as a Zondervan ebook.
Visit www.zondervan.com/ebooks.

This title is also available in a Zondervan audio edition.
Visit www.zondervan.fm.

Requests for information should be addressed to:

Zondervan, 3900 Sparks Drive SE, Grand Rapids, Michigan 49546

Library of Congress Cataloging-in-Publication Data

Wilson, Todd A., 1976 –
    Real Christian : bearing the marks of authentic faith / Todd Wilson.
      pages cm.
    ISBN 978-0-310-51583-8
    1. Character – Religious aspects – Christianity. 2. Christian life. I. Title.
BV4599.5.C45W55 2014
248.4 – dc23   2014012352

Cover design: SharpSeven Design
Interior design: David Conn

Printed in the United States of America

14 15 16 17 18 19 20 /DCI/ 21 20 19 18 17 16 15 14 13 12 11 10 9 8 7 6 5 4 3 2 1

To Tom and Julie Steller,
two of the most real Christians I know

Though we call ourselves Christians and would consider it as an affront put upon us, for anyone to doubt whether we were Christians or not; yet there are a great many who bear the name of Christ that yet do not so much as know what real Christianity is.

George Whitefield,
"Marks of a True Conversion"

CONTENTS

1

GET REAL

"We just want the old Todd back," my best friend said resentfully. The words sprung out of his mouth so easily it made me think he had little idea of the crushing blow he had just delivered. It was as though I'd stolen something from him, and he wanted it back.

Has it really come to this? I thought, as I stared back at him, not sure what to say. I'd been a Christian for only a year, and I thought I was handling my newfound faith quite well. But the frustrated look on his face indicated something different.

It was spring break of my senior year in high school, and I was supposed to be having the time of my life—a week of fun in the sun with my two buddies, a last hurrah before we finished high school and headed off to college.

But there was a problem. I wasn't who I used to be; I was different. A year earlier, in the corner booth of a McDonald's just a mile from my house, I met Jesus.

On a snowy afternoon in mid-December of 1992, a man I hardly knew told me the bad news about who I am in my sin—and the good news about who Jesus is on his cross. For about thirty minutes, this stranger shared with me the gospel story, using his coffee-stained napkin to illustrate the message with chapter and verse.

When he finished, he asked if I wanted to pray. I did, and there God entered my life.

And I began to change, so much so the people around me took notice. My mother, who at first was skeptical of my conversion, witnessed such a dramatic change in me that she concluded there must be something more to this Jesus-thing. She met Christ a year later.

And so, as I sat on the edge of the bed in a hotel where we were staying, mentally groping around for how to respond to my friend's request to return to him the old Todd, a verse of Scripture darted into my mind. This was miraculous itself, because at this point in my fledgling faith I hardly knew two verses of Scripture!

Feeling prompted, I got up and went into another room to retrieve my Bible, which I had carefully tucked away in my suitcase. I then returned, Bible in hand, and opened to one of Paul's letters.

"Guys, I want to read you something," I announced to my two friends.

They were agreeable, so I began to read, my voice quivering nervously, as I knew this was a point of no return in identifying with Jesus: "Therefore, if anyone is in Christ, he is a new creation. The old has passed away; behold, the new has come" (2 Corinthians 5:17).

It took all of ten seconds to read. When I had finished, I looked up at them anxiously, wondering how they would react to what I feared would be viewed as an original Bible thumping.

They both had blank looks on their faces; they were amazed at what just happened. But after a split moment of awkward silence, eyes darting to and fro, they looked at each other, back at me, and then one of them said, "Well, okay. I guess that says it all." We then spontaneously sprang to our feet, gave each other high fives, tossed around a few jokes to relieve the tension, as high school boys like to do when a situation gets too serious, and went about enjoying the rest of our spring break.

But I was no longer the old Todd. I had become new. I wasn't playing or pretending. There wasn't anything forced or fake about it. By the grace of God, I was real, and it was evident in my life, visible for all to see.

WHAT DOES IT MEAN TO BE REAL?

Nobody likes a fake. Even in our airbrush culture, we despise counterfeits and crave authenticity. Everyone wants to be real.

But what does it mean to be real? No one really knows. Or so it seems.

Try an experiment. Listen to people talk about what it means to be a Christian. Do you know what you will hear? Lots of competing answers and plenty of confusion.

Perhaps you recall when 2012 presidential hopeful Senator Rick Santorum claimed that President Barack Obama's policies were based on "a different theology."

Reporters, of course, pounced on this juicy piece of journalistic red meat. "Did Senator Santorum," they asked, "have the audacity, not of hope, but political incorrectness, to call into question the president's claim to be a Christian?"

When Senator Santorum was pressed, he gave a politically savvy response: "If the president says he's a Christian, he's a Christian."[1] End of story. Next question, please.

His answer satisfied reporters, and thousands of others following the story. It was as if he said, "To profess faith is to possess faith." And what could be less objectionable, or more American, than that?

But one wonders what Jesus thinks of what Santorum said.

Is it enough simply to *say* we're real, or should we be able to *see* we're real? And if so, what should we see? Are there marks of authentic faith we should see in our lives, or in the lives of others? And what about the watching world? What should they see in the lives of real Christians?

THE ANSWER TO UNCHRISTIAN

Now, more than a decade into the twenty-first century, the evangelical church faces huge challenges to its ministry and mission — radical pluralism, aggressive secularism, political polarization, skepticism about religion, revisionist sexual ethics, postmodern conceptions of truth.

But perhaps the greatest threat to the church's witness is one of our own making — *an image problem*. Many outside the church view Christians as *unchristian* in their attitudes and actions — bigoted, homophobic, hypocritical, materialistic, judgmental, self-serving, overly political. Several years ago, David Kinnaman and Gabe Lyons showed this in their book *Unchristian*, which landed like a bombshell on a happy-go-lucky evangelicalism, causing many of us to do some serious soul-searching.[2]

The evangelical church's image problem doesn't bode well for its future. In fact, the data suggests that evangelical Christianity is declining in North America. Despite the church's best efforts to appeal to the disillusioned, we continue to see alarming trends. Droves of people, especially from younger generations, are leaving the church and don't plan to return. This has driven some to predict the end of evangelicalism.[3]

The reasons for this discouraging state of affairs are complex, not cookie-cutter. But we know one thing is certain: *When Christians are confused about what it means to be real, the spiritual decline of the church will follow.*

In our increasingly post-Christian culture, where confusion about what it means to be real abounds, and where distrust of organized religion has reached an all-time high, the church needs to *get real*. We must clarify for ourselves, and for a watching world, what it means to live a life of authentic faith.

That's why I've written this book — to provide Christians with a clear and compelling description of what it means to be real. My chief claim, although provocative, is simple. *Real is something you can see.* There is a *visible difference* between real and not-real Christians. It's not enough to *say* you're real; you should be able to *see* you're real.

Being real is more than regularly attending church, feeling

good about God, or "accepting" Jesus as your Savior; it goes beyond being baptized, receiving Communion, reciting the creed, or joining in church membership. As important as these things are, being real runs deeper than these things.

Real Christians are new creatures. Physically, they won't look different than others, at least not in the way they dress or keep their hair. Yet real Christians are radically changed — they've experienced a new birth, received a new heart, and enjoy new desires. Which makes them altogether new people who live new lives.

And it shows. If you're real, it will reveal itself in your life. Real Christians bear the marks of authentic faith in ways that can be seen, heard, and felt. When you know what you're looking for, you can see the marks of real in their lives — and in your own.

THE HEART IS A FLATTERY FACTORY

Many of us lack clarity about what it means to be real. As a result, we struggle to distinguish between what's real and what's not. We are easily deceived. Jesus understands this struggle, which is why he warns, "Beware of false prophets, who come to you in sheep's clothing but inwardly are ravenous wolves" (Matthew 7:15). He knows we're easily confused and will mistake wolves for sheep. I have seven children, and we've visited the zoo countless times. But I've never seen one of them make such a simple mistake!

This struggle isn't just in discerning if *others* are real, though; we also struggle to know whether we *ourselves* are real. Even mature Christians find it hard to distinguish authentic spiritual experience from the imitations and counterfeits. What is the difference between that exciting rush you get when you sense God has spoken to you and the stimulating effect of a double espresso from Starbucks? It's surprisingly difficult to know.

And to complicate things further, we can think we're real—so can others as well—when in fact we're not. This is why Jesus must warn, "Not everyone who says to me, 'Lord, Lord,' will enter the kingdom of heaven" (Matthew 7:21). Professing Jesus as Lord doesn't mean you know Jesus as Lord.

We also confuse participating in churchy activities with genuine faith. This is why Jesus also cautions, "On that day many will say to me, 'Lord, Lord, did we not prophesy in your name, and cast out demons in your name, and do many mighty works in your name?' And then will I declare to them, 'I never knew you; depart from me, you workers of lawlessness'" (Matthew 7:22–23). Evidently, on the last day Jesus will exclude from the kingdom even some pastors and missionaries, miracle workers and Sunday school teachers, because, despite appearances, they're not real.

Here's the problem we all face: *We can convince ourselves that we're something we're not.* "The heart is deceitful above all things, and desperately sick; who can understand it?" (Jeremiah 17:9). Our depraved heart is a flattery factory, which mass-produces agreeable thoughts about ourselves at a furious pace. We lose sight of who we are and convince ourselves we're someone more attractive or cleverer or kinder than the evidence in our lives supports. Our untrustworthy hearts keep pumping self-aggrandizing compliments into our minds—leaving us comfortably reassured, yet spectacularly self-deceived.

KNOWN BY THEIR FRUIT

While Christians are confused about what it means to be real, Jesus is not. "Thus you will recognize them by their fruits," he says (Matthew 7:20). You know you're real if you bear fruit, he tells us. Fruit is the telltale sign of authentic faith because fruit doesn't lie. "For no good tree bears bad fruit, nor again does a bad tree bear good fruit, for each tree is known by its own fruit. For figs are not gathered from thornbushes, nor are grapes picked from a bramble bush" (Luke 6:43–44).

Jesus underscores this point in his famous parable about the sower (Matthew 13:1–23). The parable itself is straightforward. A farmer sows seed in a field, and the seed represents the good news of the kingdom. It is sown on four different kinds of soil, each representing a different response to the message of the kingdom. Simple enough, right? But here's the punch line: *Only one type of soil bears fruit.*

The seed sown on the first soil hardly gets started. Satan comes and snatches it away. But what's even more troubling is the outcome of the seed sown on the second and third soils. Why? Because both respond *positively* to the message, at least initially. These seeds appear to take root and begin growing into something real. Yet as the story continues, we learn that neither seed bears fruit. Neither lasts to the end, and thus neither seed is real.

Some of the seeds fail to develop roots, and they don't

persevere when life gets hard and their faith is tested. All we see from this seed is a burst of enthusiasm, but no staying power. Perhaps this is someone who got excited about fellowship or forgiveness, but lacked love for Christ. They only have the *appearance* of being real. Over time, their faith proved counterfeit.

We assume the third seed had a similarly joyful response to the message. Yet this soon dissipates because of revived interest in the things of the world—a career promotion, a new vacation home, saving toward their 401(k) plan. These concerns choke any fledgling faith, and the person falls away.

Why does Jesus tell his disciples this sobering parable? Why such a blunt story about the distinction between authentic and inauthentic responses to his message? Evidently, Jesus doesn't equate professing faith with possessing faith, as we so often do. Instead, he warns his disciples that only one thing matters—bearing fruit.

So if we are to take Jesus' challenge seriously, what should we look for in our lives?

A MASTERWORK ON SPIRITUALITY

During a difficult season in my ministry, I was encouraged by an older, wiser pastor named Jonathan Edwards (1703–1758). Although he's been dead for centuries, you may know him through his writings—a treasure trove of biblical insight and pastoral wisdom.

Considered America's greatest philosopher and theologian, Jonathan Edwards played a strategic role in the Great Awakening, a movement of the Holy Spirit that enveloped the American colonies in the 1730s and '40s. Because of the diverse and often dramatic work of the Spirit in people's lives, Edwards grappled intensely with the question we consider in this book — *What is a real Christian?*[4]

Edwards wrote several books on this topic, but his most mature thinking is found in a book titled *Religious Affections.*[5] His aim in the treatise is simple — he attempts to define the nature of true Christian experience by identifying what he calls the "twelve signs" of genuine faith.

In God's good providence, I found myself reading *Religious Affections* as part of my morning routine. Each day I would read a dozen or so pages, lingering over Edwards's observations, pondering his insights. I continued this for several years, working my way through the book, cover to cover, half a dozen times. On the title page of my copy, you'll find written in shades of blue ink, "1st reading, Sept. – Oct. 2009; 2nd reading, April 2010; 3rd and 4th reading, March – May 2011; 5th reading, Oct. 2011; 6th reading, March 2013."

Reading Edwards was invaluable. He helped me see I wasn't alone in wrestling with what it means to be a real Christian; in fact, as Edwards realized, this is *a perennial question* for the church. Each generation must wrestle with this issue and draw on the wisdom of Scripture and the saints of old to offer the church a faithful and relevant description of the marks of authentic faith.

That's why you have the book you are now holding. Following in the footsteps of Edwards, I've taken up the challenge to provide the church with a description of what it means to be a real Christian. And while I'm indebted to Edwards, this isn't an exposition of his *Religious Affections.*[6]

Instead, I've absorbed his vision but rearticulated it in terms of my own biblical reflections and pastoral experience—and in conversation with the challenges we face today.

THE STANDARD AND SUBSTANCE OF AUTHENTICITY

As I mentioned earlier, Edwards identified twelve marks of authentic faith. I have cut that number in half, simplifying when necessary, consolidating where possible, to distill his twelve down to six: *humility, meekness, contrition, wholeness, hunger,* and *perfected love.*

These six marks provide us with the standard and substance of authentic faith. On the one hand, they provide a biblical *standard* for whether we are real; on the other hand, they unpack the *substance* of what mature faith looks like. They give us criteria for testing ourselves to see whether, or in what ways, God is working in our lives. But they also define the content of what a mature Christian looks like, to help us see what characteristics should mark the life of a real and authentic disciple of Jesus.[7]

The good news about these marks is that you never outgrow them. The six qualities we discuss in this book are the stuff of authentic faith, the heart and soul of the Christian life, and they provide a starting point to know whether we're real. We never move beyond them; we only go deeper in each of them. So whether you're curious as to what an authentic Christian is or interested in what it means to further grow in your relationship with Christ, this book should speak to you.

BEING REAL IS MORE THAN RIGHT BELIEF OR RADICAL BEHAVIOR

If you surf blogs, read books, or attend Christian conferences, you will likely hear many Christian leaders calling for the church to "get real." And while I say amen to their intent, I find myself questioning what they emphasize. Some will say that *right belief* is the key to reclaiming authentic Christianity. These thoughtful (and often young) folks are restless to see the writings of Reformed theologians in everyone's personal library. Less fluff, more doctrine is what we need to get real.[8]

Others are just as convinced that *radical behavior* is the telltale sign of genuine faith. For these eager souls, it's all about being sold-out for Jesus. Enough of orthodoxy, or right thinking; we need more orthopraxy, or right living. Forget seminary. If you want to be a real Christian, go start a soup kitchen.[9]

The truth is that our churches need a double portion of both of these. On the one hand, biblical literacy and theological understanding are at historically low levels, giving rise to an outbreak of "bad religion" in America today.[10] On the other hand, an increasingly marginalized church needs to regain credibility by putting its faith into practice rather than simply rehearsing the same old slogans and banal clichés as we watch Rome burn.

Of course, this isn't an either/or debate. You can't have real faith without right beliefs because the Christian faith is rooted in truth. Nor can you follow Jesus and fail to live radically—denying yourself, taking up your cross, and following the Lamb wherever he goes (see Revelation 14:4).

Yet far too often we reduce authentic faith to a litmus test of either right beliefs or radical behavior, or some arbitrary combination of the two. As important as they both are, neither one of them guarantees you're real. What did James, the Lord's brother, say? Even demons know doctrine—they just don't love Jesus (see James 2:19). And what was Paul's caution? You can be radical—even give your body to the flames—yet not have love, and thus fail to be real (see 1 Corinthians 13:3).

Being real, then, isn't just about having your mind informed by biblical truth or your behavior conformed to Christ's standards; it's about seeing your life *transformed* by the power of the Holy Spirit. Let me be clear. Doctrine is essential; so, too, is radical behavior—the one is a prerequisite, the other a necessary overflow. But the source and seed of real Christianity stand between these two, between right belief and radical behavior.[11]

Transformed character is where we see Christ in the lives of Christians. It's the one thing you can't fake, because only real Christians are being conformed into the image of Christ.

THE JOY OF BEING REAL

Let me invite you, then, to explore what it means to be a real Christian. There's no more pressing question you can answer than knowing whether you're right with God—and few things are sweeter than an *assurance of salvation*. Most Christians believe they can and should know whether they're real, but few are prepared to tell you how or why.

Hopefully, as you read this book, you'll take a good, hard look at yourself. I trust many will be encouraged by what they read, and that you personally will see evidence that you are real—and have reason to rejoice!

Others, however, may find reading this difficult, even unsettling. You've always thought you were real, but you may realize the evidence just isn't there. Regardless of where you are spiritually, however, I encourage you to be honest with yourself in this process, because it's always better to arrive at a place of clarity than to persist in a state of confusion, especially when it comes to questions about your own soul.

Perhaps you'll find it helpful to read this book with a spouse or friend, or discuss it together in a small group. That kind of encouragement is beneficial when wrestling with an important topic. To assist in this process, you'll find resources at the end of each chapter to help you explore the marks of a real Christian. There are questions for reflection to be used on your own or in a group, a selection of Scripture passages that deal with the mark being considered, suggestions for further reading if you'd like to dig deeper into one of the marks, and a few biographies of people who have embodied one of the marks of a real Christian in a powerful way.

As you gain clarity about what it means to be real, I'm confident you'll also be better equipped to recognize the difference between what's real and what's not—whether in your life or in someone else's. *Increased spiritual discernment* is my second aim with this book, not so you become a spiritual cop, a Pharisee in your church, a know-it-all who presumes to see what God alone can see—the state of another's heart; rather, my hope is that you will learn to navigate your way through these confusing times in which we live, when counterfeits abound.

I pray this book also *increases your joy* by giving you a new appreciation for the power of the gospel and the wonder of God's grace. "For by grace you have been saved through faith," Paul reminds us, "it is the gift of God" (Ephesians 2:8). I hope you'll see that being real isn't routine; it's marvelous! What do we see when we see the marks of real in our lives? The marks of real *reveal the life of God in your life*. When you see humility or meekness or contrition or wholeness or hunger or perfected love in your life, you see the risen Christ at work. "It is no longer I who live," you will say with Paul, "but Christ who lives in me" (Galatians 2:20). This isn't self-wrought sanctification or performance-oriented Christianity, but gospel-rooted, Spirit-empowered living for Jesus' sake!

I've written this book to help you make the truth about Jesus visible so others can see him in your life. A man once met Amy Carmichael, missionary to India, and asked her, "Can you show us the life of your Lord Jesus?" Many in our day of disillusionment are asking this same question but are seldom finding a convincing answer. Real Christians, however, who by God's grace bear the marks of authentic faith, reveal the life of Christ to a watching world.

What could be more thrilling than that?

CHAPTER RESOURCES

QUESTIONS FOR REFLECTION

1. Before reading this chapter, what would you have said were the marks of authentic faith?

2. The author says that "when Christians are confused about what it means to be real, the spiritual decline of the church will follow." Do you agree? Why might that be the case?

3. How would getting real about what it means to have authentic faith help address what the author refers to as Christianity's image problem?

4. Read the parable of the sower (Matthew 13:1–23). What happens to the seed sown among the various soils? Reflect on Jesus' explanation. Why do you think Jesus tells this parable?

5. "The heart is deceitful above all things" (Jeremiah 17:9). In what ways are we deceived about our own spiritual condition? Why is that?

6. Take a look at 2 Corinthians 13:5. Why does the apostle Paul call us to examine ourselves? How do we do that?

SCRIPTURES TO PONDER

- Matthew 5–7
- 2 Corinthians 10–12
- 2 Peter
- Jude

BOOKS TO HELP YOU DIG DEEPER

Edwards, Jonathan. *The Works of Jonathan Edwards, Volume 2: Religious Affections*. Edited by John E. Smith. 1959. Reprint, New Haven, CT: Yale University Press, 2009.

Idleman, Kyle. *Not a Fan: Becoming a Completely Committed Follower of Jesus*. Grand Rapids: Zondervan, 2011.

Platt, David. *Follow Me: A Call to Die. A Call to Live*. Downers Grove, IL: Tyndale, 2013.

Wilberforce, William, *Real Christianity*. Revised and updated by Bob Beltz. Ventura, CA: Regal, 2006.

Biographies for Encouragement

Aitken, Jonathan. *Charles W. Colson: A Life Redeemed*. Colorado Springs: WaterBrook, 2005.

Marsden, George M. *A Short Life of Jonathan Edwards*. Grand Rapids: Eerdmans, 2008.

2

CHRISTIANS WITHOUT CHESTS?

Before we look closely at the six marks of authentic faith, we need to talk about the heart — not the organ in your chest that pumps blood, but the center of the human person, the wellspring of our actions, the foundation of our character. We need to look at the heart for one simple reason: Before we can *be* real, we need to *become* real. Before we can bear the marks of authentic faith, we must receive a new heart. A transformed heart is what gives rise to all the marks of real — from humility to hunger. And nothing else but a new heart can do this.

C. S. Lewis coined a wonderful phrase to critique education that doesn't enliven the heart. When you teach only to inform minds but fail to ignite feelings, you run the risk of creating, Lewis says, "men without chests." Your students will be all intellect or appetite, but have no heart — little Mr. Spocks or Hugh Hefners. They'll be nothing more than urban blockheads or trousered apes.[12]

Lewis saw this as infecting education in his day, but we have reason to suspect it's gone viral within evangelical Christianity today. Everywhere we see signs of our neglect of the heart; in fact, we've raised a generation of *Christians without chests*—church folks who want authentic faith, but lack a new heart.

As a pastor, I often find myself sitting with people in their living room or in my study as they unpack a broken relationship or confess a pattern of sin. They want counseling because life has gone to pot. Their marriage is in shambles; their computer is full of pornography; or they've dispensed with church and their spouse is worried to the point of not eating.

Sometimes, these conversations go well. The person acknowledges where they have hurt others or where they have loved someone or something more than God, and we talk about what needs to change, ask God for forgiveness, and pray for the grace to live as they truly want—to "walk in newness of life" (Romans 6:4).

Other times, though, these conversations don't go well at all. The person grows defensive and resentful, or is simply unwilling to hear the truth of God's Word. But how *can* they, if they lack the ability to do so? Christians without chests—those who lack a new heart—don't have what they need to do what it is they know they should do. Their heads can be filled with all the right beliefs, their calendars with all the right activities, but they lack that vital link between what they believe and what they do. They often look real, but sadly there's nothing of real spiritual life inside their soul, in that place the Bible calls the heart.

Listen to how friends describe what it means to be a

Christian or how you become a Christian, and you'll see what I mean. Do you know what will be conspicuously absent? Any mention of the reality of the heart.

I've heard people talk about a person who got saved, yet fail to consider whether that person has received a new heart—as though all you have to do is "decide" for Christ and—voilà!—you're real. Or you will sometimes hear people share how they've grown in Christ, yet not mention anything about how their desires have changed, as though Christian maturity were only about increased biblical understanding or churchly activities. Sometimes I will hear people evaluate worship by commenting on the atmosphere in the auditorium or the arrangement of the music rather than whether or not their heart was hungry for the truth and united with the person of Christ. Or we hear well-meaning Christians evaluate preaching as if it were only about communicating information or providing application—an easy-to-follow message with a few bits of practical takeaway—with no concern for whether the preaching has moved them to love Jesus more.

These are just a few examples, but can you begin to see what's missing in all of this? Any mention of the heart, of the new taste they have for spiritual things or the new eyes they have that are drawn to the beauty of Christ. Many people just assume you can be a real Christian without these things.

I'm convinced that this widespread neglect of the heart explains the lack of vitality we often find in our churches today. Could this be why evangelical Christianity seems spiritually anemic? Studies consistently show that self-identified born-again Christians are on a par with society in the rate of divorce, use of pornography, lack of charitable giving, and racial prejudice. Could our churches be filled with professing Christians who lack new hearts?

THE CENTRALITY OF THE HEART

If we open our Bibles, it is hard to miss the importance of the heart. Scripture *always* places the heart at the center of what it means to be real. It's never peripheral. Just open your Bible and see what it says.

Every time the Bible defines what it means to be an authentic Christian, it speaks in the language of the heart—about the heart, to the heart. And anytime the Bible calls you to a life of faith, your heart is being summoned to a vital response to the living Christ.

The Bible calls believers to fear God (Ecclesiastes 12:13), to strive to be zealous for his name (Romans 12:11), and to hope in his promises (Psalm 42:5). The Bible describes real Christians as those who seek the Lord (1 Chronicles 16:11), grieve over their sin (Psalm 51:1–9), mourn the plight of the lost (Matthew 23:37), and lament the reality of sickness, disease, and death (Romans 8:22–23). The Bible invites us to give thanks to the Lord (Psalm 9:1), rejoice with singing (Psalm 33:1–3), and worship him with gladness (Psalm 100:2). The Bible exhorts us to have compassion (Colossians 3:12), show mercy (Micah 6:8), and be generous (Hebrews 13:16). And the Bible calls us to love both God and our neighbor (Luke 10:27)—all of which flow from the heart.

If we want convincing proof that the heart is central to what it means to be real, we need only to look closely at the life of our Savior. For nowhere does real Christianity come into sharper focus than in the person of Jesus. And what do we find? A heart ablaze for the glory of God: "I glorified you on earth, having accomplished the work that you gave me to do. And now, Father, glorify me in your own presence with the glory that I had with you before the world existed" (John 17:4–5). We see Jesus consumed with a desire to do the Father's will: "My food is to do the will of him who sent me and to accomplish his work" (John 4:34). We see his heart yielded to his Father's good pleasure: "My soul is very sorrowful, even to death ... Abba, Father, all things are possible for you. Remove this cup from me. Yet not what I will, but what you will" (Mark 14:34, 36). And we see him zealous for the Father's honor: "Take these things away; do not make my Father's house a house of trade" (John 2:16).

If we learn anything from the pages of Scripture about the life of our Savior, it's that the heart is at the center of who he is.[13] Everything Jesus did flowed from his heart—a wellspring of desire to honor his heavenly Father. Should it be any different for us? If it's true of Jesus, ought it not be true for you and me—for those of us who seek to model our lives after his, authentically following in his footsteps, claiming to have his life indwelling our own?

TWICE-BORN

The heart is at the center of what it means to be real because from it flow the marks of real. Unless you've been given a new heart, you're going nowhere spiritually. But how do we get this new heart? According to Jesus, it is not something we can earn or something we can work for—not something God owes to us. It must be given to us as a gift. Jesus puts it this way: We must be *born again*. Jesus agrees with the old adage—there are only two types of people in the world: those who've been born once, and those who've been born twice. The twice-born, they're real; the once-born, they're not.[14]

It may strike you as quaint or even bizarre to talk about being twice-born. It sounded curious to a man named Nicodemus, as he heard Jesus insist that if you want to be real, you must be twice-born. "Truly, truly, I say to you, unless one is born again he cannot see the kingdom of God" (John 3:3).

Nicodemus was baffled by what Jesus said, but not because Nicodemus was unschooled or irreligious. He was a very learned, pious, and devout Jew. No, it was only because Nicodemus had never heard anything like this before.

"How can a man be born when he is old?" Nicodemus asked. "Can he enter a second time into his mother's womb and be born?" (John 3:4).

Rather than answer his question, Jesus restated a most shocking truth for Nicodemus—one that should be equally shocking for us as well: "Truly, truly, I say to you, unless one is born of water and the Spirit, he cannot enter the kingdom of God" (John 3:5). We are born once by water. That's our natural birth, and everyone shares in that. But we must also be born by the Spirit—a supernatural birth!

DIVINE RESIDENT

New birth marks the beginning of a real Christian life because that is when God's Spirit comes to dwell within you. During his earthly ministry, Jesus encouraged his disciples with the promise that the Father was going to send them "another Helper, to be with you forever, even the Spirit of truth, whom the world cannot receive, because it neither sees him nor knows him" (John 14:16–17). The world, Jesus says, remains oblivious of this—dead to the presence of the Spirit. But not so for those who are real. As Jesus points out, "You know him, for he dwells with you and will be in you" (John 14:17).

When you're born again, something remarkable happens—the Holy Spirit takes up residence within you. In fact, he takes possession of you and assumes the title deed to your soul. He moves into your heart and begins making himself at home in your life. On the other hand, if you're not born again, the Spirit doesn't live within you. He may visit you from time to time, occasionally rent a room from you, park his car outside your house, send you text messages or an occasional Christmas card. But there's a wide difference between the Spirit *acting* on you in these ways and the Spirit *dwelling* in you deeply and permanently, transforming your life.

During our late twenties, my wife, Katie, and I moved each summer over a period of five years. Every time, we had to pack up our entire home and endure constant transitions. Because we were constantly moving, we developed some expertise in packing and unpacking stuff. We refined the art (and science) of moving into a new home quickly and efficiently. In fact, we became so adept at moving into new places that we would have the furniture arranged, dishes put away, and pictures hung before we went to bed the first night! We didn't waste any time moving into our new home.

When we are born again, the Spirit becomes a divine resident in our heart. When he moves into our lives, he immediately gets to work, makes the place his own, and changes stuff about who we are and how we live so that it better matches who he is and how he lives. Little by little, over time, we begin to see our lives transformed by his presence. Over time, everyone should be able to tell that someone else is living in the home of our heart.

MARKED BY THE SPIRIT

This is the experience of all real Christians—the Spirit turns you into what he likes, not by removing your personality, but by renewing your character. The Spirit makes his character, your character; his holiness, yours. Until one day, the change is complete and your character perfectly matches his. In your desires, drives, and thoughts, you will resemble the Son, who is the perfect image of the Father.

In this way, God marks you as belonging to him. The Bible refers to this as the "sealing" of the Spirit (2 Corinthians 1:22; Ephesians 1:13). In the ancient world, a king or dignitary would impress his image on hot wax to verify that a letter was his. So, too, the King of heaven impresses his image, not on hot wax, but on your life, so that it's clear you belong to him and not to another. This is the King's verification of you, his certification of your authenticity. God stamps his own image on you—your heart, your soul, and your character. As your life is made holy by the Holy Spirit, you increasingly display that image. And this is how, as Paul says, the Spirit "bears witness with our spirit that we are children of God" (Romans 8:16). Like a lawyer arguing his case in a courtroom, the Holy Spirit marshals evidence to prove to the world that you're real.

But what evidence does the Spirit use to make his case? *He uses the change he himself makes in your life.* This is the compelling evidence that you're real. In other words, the Spirit points to his own fruit — the "fruit of the Spirit" (Galatians 5:22 – 23) — which he himself has caused to grow in your life. And as he exerts himself, leading you in the path of love, joy, peace, patience, kindness, and so on, he demonstrates to you that you're real, that you belong to God. "For all who are led by the Spirit of God are sons of God" (Romans 8:14).

What matters, then, is that your life is being transformed, not just in what you believe or what you do, but in your character. The Spirit changes you, your desires and drives, making the first commandment first in your heart. The Spirit may give you his gifts, but the real question is, Has he given you his *grace*, the grace that saves and sanctifies you, making you holy? You may speak in tongues of men and of angels, have prophetic powers, understand all mysteries and all knowledge, possess a faith that moves mountains, be willing to give all you have, even embrace martyrdom (see 1 Corinthians 13:1 – 3). But at the end of the day, the only question that matters is this: Do you have divine love dwelling in your soul? Has God shed his love abroad in your heart by the Holy Spirit (Romans 5:5)?

NICE PEOPLE OR NEW MEN — REVISITED

To be twice-born, born again by the Spirit, is a remarkable thing. It is a miracle of God's grace. Sadly, the experience of being "born again" has become something of a cliché in our day, and we don't stop to ask what it really means. If we let Scripture guide our understanding, we realize that the new birth is glorious and has profound implications for our lives and for the church. I'll close this chapter by considering a few of these.*

First, although you're still you, the new birth makes you entirely new. Real Christians are a different kind of creature, set apart from all other human beings. The difference is one of kind, not simply of degree. A real Christian isn't merely a cleaned-up version of a non-Christian, but a new creature—radically different by virtue of new birth.

Second, although you're entirely new, you may not be nicer than those who aren't new. Just because you're real, it doesn't mean you'll be nicer, in every respect, than someone who's not real. What you need to remember is that God begins re-creating you by starting where you are and with who you are. And let's face it, some of us start off in worse shape than others! So the question is not, Are you nicer than every non-Christian? The question is, Are you nicer, or more Christlike, than you would be without Christ?[15]

Third, although you're born again at a specific moment in time, the evidence of new birth is best seen only over an extended period of time. You're not born again over time, as though this new birth were a slow, steady process. The new birth is an event, not a process. But it still takes time to detect your "spiritual vitals," those reliable signs of new spiritual life. The Spirit transforms us in different ways and at different speeds;

---

* In this section I take inspiration from and draw on the wonderful insights of C. S. Lewis in *Mere Christianity*, in his chapter in book IV titled "Nice People or New Men" (1952; repr., New York: Macmillan, 1960), 174–83.

no one's transformation will be identical to anyone else's. God has a unique way of dealing with each of his children.

Fourth, although your salvation doesn't depend on the evidences of new birth, if there is no evidence in your life, you have no reason to think you're either saved or born again. To be born again is to experience a profound change, a fundamental alteration of who you are. "Therefore, if anyone is in Christ," Paul writes to the Corinthians, "he is a new creation. The old has passed away; behold, the new has come" (2 Corinthians 5:17). If the desires of your heart and the direction of your life have not changed, then you have no reason to assume you're born again.

And let me hasten to add, this change must be substantive, not superficial. It must be real change, to the core of who you are — your heart — reshaping the direction of your life, your motivations, and your actions.

If you're real, this change will also be permanent, not temporary. Even a pig can be cleaned up for a party. But as the apostle Peter says, those moral reforms won't last if the nature of that creature hasn't been changed, "The dog returns to its own vomit, and the sow, after washing herself, returns to wallow in the mire" (2 Peter 2:22).

Before you were converted, you may have struggled with a particular sin. And chances are now, even after your conversion, you still struggle with this same sin and its attendant vices. But new birth means this sin will have lost its controlling power; it will no longer dominate your life as it once did. This doesn't mean, of course, that you'll reach perfection overnight. But it does mean you'll see progress over a lifetime—even if it's oftentimes two steps forward, one step back.

Fifth, although you must be born again, you cannot give yourself new birth. I've mentioned this several times already, but it is worth repeating. Spiritual rebirth isn't within our control. We can't order it online or find it at the grocery store. It's not something you purchase at the drugstore, borrow from a friend, or inherit from a deceased aunt. Remember Jesus' words to Nicodemus: "That which is born of the flesh is flesh, and that which is born of the Spirit is spirit" (John 3:6).

Flesh only gives birth to flesh. It may be more refined, prettier, and even nicer flesh in some ways. But it's still flesh—dead to God and condemned to be judged as a consequence of sin. Apart from the Spirit, you'll never be anything other than flesh.

But recall Jesus' words about the mysterious moving of the Spirit: "The wind blows where it wishes, and you hear its sound, but you do not know where it comes from or where it goes. So it is with everyone who is born of the Spirit" (John 3:8). You and I can no more control the Spirit than we can catch the wind. He is sovereign in salvation and gives new birth to whomever he pleases.

"I MUST BE BORN AGAIN, OR BE DAMNED!"

George Whitefield, the leading evangelist of the First Great Awakening in the mid-1700s in America and Great Britain, became the remarkable man he was through a startling realization. As a student at Oxford, Whitefield came across a small book written by a Scottish pastor named Henry Scougal. The book has an inviting title, *The Life of God in the Soul of Man*. So Whitefield picked it up and read it intently.

This small book rocked his world. As he read Scougal's words, Whitefield came face-to-face with the question we are considering in this book: *What does it mean to be real?* Whitefield saw how the Bible defines authentic faith—and how this definition was at odds with what he had thought being a real Christian was all about. Listen to him describe this life-altering experience:

> God showed me that I must be born again, or be damned! I learned that a man may go to church, say his prayers, receive the sacrament, and yet not be a Christian. How did my heart rise and shudder, like a poor man that is afraid to look into his account-books, lest he should find himself a bankrupt.
>
> "Shall I burn this book? Shall I throw it down? Or shall I search it?" I did search it; and, holding the book in my hand, thus addressed the God of heaven and earth: "Lord, if I am not a Christian, or if I am not *a real one*, for Jesus Christ's sake, show me what Christianity is that I may not be damned at last!"
>
> God soon showed me, for in reading a few lines further, that, "true religion is a union of the soul with God, and Christ formed within us," a ray of Divine light was instantaneously darted in upon my soul, and from that moment, but not till then, did I know that I must become a new creature.[16]

Real Christians are *new* creatures. Regular church attendance, religious devotions, sharing in the sacraments—these don't make you a Christian, at least, as Whitefield realized, not a real one. If you want to be real, or bear the marks of authentic faith, you must be born again.

Perhaps you have never heard anyone talk about being "born again" before. Or you've never thought about what actually makes a person a Christian. Before we continue into the next chapter, I'd like to invite you to pause and ask yourself a question: *Am I a real Christian? Not because of church attendance or a profession of faith, but because of new birth? Have I been born again?*

You may need to set this book down and spend some time praying, talking to God, being honest with him about the state of your heart and soul. Ask God to show you if you're not a real Christian — and to help you see, perhaps for the first time, why you need Jesus, why his life, death, and resurrection is for you. "Believe in the Lord Jesus, and you will be saved," is the scriptural formula (Acts 16:31). Ask God to give you faith, to change and transform your heart — giving you a desire to know, love, and trust Jesus.

And as you do so, may divine light dart in upon your soul — even now!

CHAPTER RESOURCES

QUESTIONS FOR REFLECTION

1. In your own words, what does it mean to be a Christian "without a chest"? How would you describe such a person? Do you know anyone like this? Are you a Christian without a chest?

2. Read Ezekiel 36:16 – 32. In verses 24 – 26, Ezekiel declares the gift of a new heart as God's saving solution for sinful people. Why is the heart critical in someone's salvation experience?

3. Consider King David, that "man after God's own heart" (1 Samuel 13:14; Acts 13:22). Why can't you call yourself a real Christian if you ignore the reality of the heart?

4. Consider the example of Jesus. We learn that the heart is at the heart of who he is. See Matthew 11:28 – 29; Mark 14:34; Luke 13:34; John 2:16; 4:34; 11:33 – 35; 13:1; 17:4 – 5. What does it mean for the heart to be at the heart of what it means to be real?

5. What is the relationship between the heart and spiritual activity and disciplines?

6. Describe how your heart has been stirred by reading this chapter. As you consider your heart before God, how might other believers serve as an encouragement to you?

SCRIPTURES TO PONDER

- Jeremiah 31:31 – 34
- Ezekiel 36:16 – 32
- John 3
- Romans 3 – 8

BOOKS TO HELP YOU DIG DEEPER

Greear, J. D. *Stop Asking Jesus into Your Heart*. Nashville: Broadman & Holman, 2013.

Piper, John. *Finally Alive!* Fearn, Ross-shire, Scotland: Christian Focus, 2009.

Scougal, Henry. *The Life of God in the Soul of Man*. Philadelphia: Westminster, 1948.

Biographies for Encouragement

Colson, Charles. *Born Again*. New York: Bantam, 1976.

Dallimore, Arnold A. *George Whitefield: The Life and Times of the Greatest Evangelist of the Eighteenth-Century Revival*. Volume 1. Edinburgh: Banner of Truth, 1980.

3
HUMILITY: TRANSCENDENT SELF-CONFIDENCE

Several years ago, I was finishing up PhD studies and preparing to leave the place that had been my home for the past three years in Cambridge, England. Some friends invited me for a farewell dinner. They also invited another friend of theirs, an independently wealthy, quintessentially British gentleman who was bright, articulate, well-read, witty, and sported a rather posh accent. Naturally, he was curious as to what I was going to do after my graduation.

"So, what are your plans?" he asked.

Since I was about to earn a PhD from one of the world's top universities, he assumed I would be heading for a teaching post at an Ivy League school—Harvard, Yale, Princeton, perhaps?

"I'm going to be a pastor," I told him, somewhat sheepishly. "P-a-s-t-o-r"—I can still hear the sound of that strange little word proceed from my mouth; it nearly got stuck on the way out, as if it didn't want to be seen or heard.

My announcement surprised the dinner guest. In fact, he looked at me incredulously, as if I had morphed into one of those ghoulish creatures from a cheap sci-fi movie. The look on his face told me I had some explaining to do—at least if I wanted to hold on to an ounce of self-respect.

I began to describe where we would live in Wheaton, Illinois, a lovely town in what Americans call the Midwest, part of that large stretch of land between New York and Los Angeles. "You know, with all those red states," I editorialized, adding a touch of humor—"where buffalo still roam." My feeble attempt failed, and he continued to stare at me disbelievingly.

So I went on to unpack what it meant to be a pastor. Evidently, he'd never met one. "A pastor," I explained, "is someone who works at this thing called a church."

On and on I continued, until his bemusement gave way to amusement, and I watched as a cheeky grin took shape on his face—it was a smirk, really. It was as if he'd finally realized what sort of creature he was talking to.

He then dipped his head so his nose was strategically pointed down at me, peered over the top of his glasses, and said in a notably condescending tone, "The pastorate? Don't you think that's a bit anticlimactic coming from Cambridge?"

Anticlimactic. Few words strike greater fear in a proud soul. Who wants their life to be anticlimactic? I felt quite small, almost silly, at that moment. In an instant, my self-worth was crushed like the ground pepper on the table before me. At the same time, I could feel the desire to defend myself surging within me. I despised being belittled and wanted to dodge or deflect the embarrassment of what it meant for me to follow Jesus.

Even worse, his comment made me doubt myself. *What am I doing going into the ministry?* I thought. *Why waste all that education? Why squander the opportunity of a promising career as a scholar, lecturer, and writer?*

I was like a drowning man groping for a life preserver, clinging to the prerogatives and prestige of my Cambridge PhD. I watched as it slipped away, leaving me to sink under the weight of my own vanity and pride. It was a humbling experience, and it didn't feel all that good.

MR. MILQUETOAST AND OTHER MISCONCEPTIONS

Let's face it, humility is hard—not like calculus, more like sacrifice. It pains the soul. No one grows in humility quickly or easily, nor do we gain it naturally. Humility cuts against the grain of human nature, and that *always* hurts.

Humility is also hard to define. It's often misunderstood, even by thoughtful, godly Christians. We tend to equate humility with certain personality types—the shy, quiet, passive, and reserved folk. But that's not what humility is really about, at least not biblically. Being a real Mr. Milquetoast, with a limp, squid handshake, doesn't mean you're humble.

Sometimes, we confuse humility with self-doubt or self-deprecation, as though, in the words of C. S. Lewis, humility involves being "a sort of greasy, smarmy person, who is always telling you that, of course, he is nobody."[17] But thinking poorly of yourself doesn't necessarily mean you're humble. In fact, self-deprecation can be a subtle species of pride.

I once attended a lecture given by a world-class biblical

scholar. The auditorium was packed, and the talk riveting. Following the presentation came the customary time for Q&A, and I noticed a fellow graduate student who shot his hand in the air to ask the first question. He began with a curious throat-clearing exercise. Then he launched into his question with an affectation to his voice, sounding like a cross between James Earl Jones and Ian McKellen. "Professor So-and-So, I would like to thank you," he began, "for providing so rich and marvelous a fare to so frail and feeble a mind." On he continued for several minutes before arriving at a rather boring question, which he'd successfully coiffed and perfumed with a blather of words that did little to conceal his self-admiring attitude.

No, humility doesn't mean putting on airs or affecting a humble demeanor. Nor do you achieve humility by pretending to be something you're not. To be humble, you don't have to convince yourself you're someone you aren't. You can be honest about your gifts and talents, and be grateful for the experiences and opportunities God has given you.

Contrary to popular opinion, humility doesn't force you to make a dozen downward adjustments in the way you view yourself. You don't need to downplay the fact that you aced the SAT or took home a fistful of firsts at the state swim meet. You don't need to hide the fact that you graduated summa cum laude from Harvard, or that you can play the cello like Yo-Yo Ma, write poetry like Goethe, have an uncanny ability to remember names, run a Fortune 500 company, or enjoy hauntingly beautiful blue eyes with thick, dark eyelashes.

The good news is that being humble doesn't require you to deny reality.

Lowly Thoughts of Self Isn't Humility

It is worth mentioning, however, that there is a long-standing and venerable tradition of Christian teaching on humility that places the emphasis precisely here. Some writers have taught, mistakenly, that to be humble is to think of yourself as lowly as possible.

One of the most influential Christians biographies ever written was by that eminent theologian I mentioned earlier, Jonathan Edwards. He wrote a biography about a young man named David Brainerd, a missionary to the Native Americans. Brainerd was by all accounts a godly individual. And the story of his life, as told by Edwards, is as challenging as it is inspiring.

I read Brainerd's biography after I had graduated from college and was moved by his life of spirituality and sacrifice. But I also came away with mixed feelings—specifically, I didn't like the way Brainerd thought about himself. I recalled a story when Brainerd entered a room full of people, and he wrote that he was overwhelmed with the sense that he was the most miserable sinner in the room. But surely the reality was much different—no doubt, Brainerd was one of the most saintly!

In short, I couldn't help but think that David Brainerd, for all his saintly qualities, was unjustifiably self-deprecating—in a way that didn't correspond to reality. I wondered if his understanding of humility—to think of oneself as lowly as possible—might be wrong. After all, it takes an impossible set of mental gymnastics to convince yourself that you're someone you're not. Or worse, it means believing something untrue about yourself.[18]

Humility Isn't Status Conscious

If humility isn't thinking you're something you are not, then what is it? I believe that when understood in the light of biblical teaching, humility is not letting who you are hinder you from loving others. *In other words, the purpose of humility isn't to make you think less of who you are, but to enable you to love others regardless of who they are.*

Humility is how love expresses itself toward those of a different status, rank, or position. It's the capacity to view everyone as *ultimately equal.* Again, this doesn't mean denying differences between people. But it does mean looking past those differences to the underlying equality of all people.

There are two important senses in which we are all equal—as creatures made in God's image, and as fallen creatures in need of God's grace. These two facts, in turn, are the foundation for true humility, because they radically level the playing field. To be sure, it's critical that we recognize our sinfulness if we want to cultivate humility, not because this leads us to conclude that we're actually *more* sinful than anyone else, but because this undercuts the temptation to think we're more entitled to receive love, or less obligated to show love to others, because of some distinctive quality we possess.

To the humble it matters little whether a person is better educated or less attractive or more accomplished. They don't experience that forlorn feeling that comes from knowing they're not as successful as someone else. Nor are they prone to get a buzz from knowing they've done something that causes them to stand out from the crowd. In fact, a humble person views another's victory as though it were his or her own.

Humility is delightfully self-forgetful. The humble don't fret over their own prestige or position, or that of others. In short, *humility is transcendent self-confidence*—a quality of character that liberates a person from having to compare themselves with others and frees them to love everyone equally.[19]

Pride is opposed to humility because pride fixates on status. The proud are always status conscious, calculating their own standing in every situation. When proud people step into a room, or meet someone new, their minds are immediately flooded with status-oriented thoughts:

"Is she more attractive than I am? Everyone does seem to be paying attention to her."

"Boy, he's articulate. I wonder if he's smarter than me."

"I bet I've got a better job than him—at least one that pays more."

"She's probably not as good of a mother as me, despite what our friends think."

The Bible provides us with a picture of how pride works in a man named Simon the Pharisee. We read about him in Luke's gospel (7:36–50). Simon invites Jesus to his house for a meal, but a woman bursts onto the scene and begins attending to Jesus, weeping at his feet and wiping them with her hair. Simon is aghast at what he sees.

From Simon's standpoint, there are at least a half dozen problems with what is happening. First of all, this is *his* house, not the woman's. It's a dinner party for his important guests, not a time for needy people to intrude with their problems. Jesus is a recognized rabbi, not a local pub owner, and rabbis don't kibitz with sinners. She's obviously a woman, and he's obviously a man, which means she shouldn't touch him, not even his feet. And worst of all, she's a recognized sinner!

No wonder Simon gasps when he sees how Jesus responds to the woman. Listen to what he mutters under his breath: "If this man were a prophet, he would have known *who* and *what sort* of woman this is who is touching him, for she is a sinner" (Luke 7:39, emphasis added). Here we see the heart of pride. Pride says, "I don't need to love you because of *who* you are." Pride impedes the flow of love because it's always taking into account another's social standing—Who are they? How do they rank in the world? Which rung do they occupy on the social ladder?

This is why pride is so damaging to love, whether of God or your neighbor. For the proud heart isn't a broken heart, but a bottled-up heart from which love can't flow. If we're preoccupied with who people are or where they stand in the world's pecking order, we will be blind to those of a different status and fail to love them as we ought.

Humility, however, doesn't cling to rights or prerogatives. And thus it clears the way for love to flow to the Savior, and then to others. Love is the goal, not humility. Humility is simply the mind-set needed to love others as God calls us to love.

THE MIND OF CHRIST

Evidently, you can occupy the top rung on the status ladder, yet be humble. In fact, you can even be completely sinless, yet entirely humble. Consider Jesus—matchless in dignity, and consummately humble. Recall the apostle Paul's description of the mind we see in Christ:

Have this mind among yourselves, which is yours in Christ Jesus, who, though he was in the form of God, did not count equality with God a thing to be grasped, but emptied himself, by taking the form of a servant, being born in the likeness of men. And being found in human form, he humbled himself by becoming obedient to the point of death, even death on a cross.

Philippians 2:5 – 8

Humility, then, is having the mind of Christ, which means *not holding on to status in a way that hinders love.* It means letting go of your own prerogatives. You can't cling to your rights or rank or standing as a reason for failing to love someone. Humility is love freely flowing among people of different positions.

This is what we see in the Son. He didn't let his own divine status hinder him from meeting the needs of sinful humanity. Instead, in humility he pressed beyond his exalted place for the sake of love. More than that, he became a human being who would die the most ignoble of deaths — death on a cross, as a tried and condemned criminal. And yet it was his humility — not counting his rights and privileges as something to use for himself — that enabled him to meet the needs of sinful human beings like you and me.

And we, Paul says in this same passage, are to do the same. Rather than being eaten up by rivalry and conceit, or envying and jockeying for pride of place, we ought in humility to "count others more significant" than ourselves (Philippians 2:3). This means looking not only to our own interests, but also to the interests of others — regardless of who they are. And when this happens, we embody humility and exhibit the mind of Christ (verse 5).

WORLDLY GRIEF AND FALSE HUMILITY

In the summer of 1999, my wife, Katie, and I led a team of college students on a mission trip to Thailand and China. One of the more fascinating parts of the trip was meandering around the streets of Bangkok, Thailand. There vendors were selling imitation goods, counterfeits made to look like the real thing. No one was selling imitations of junk—these were copies of the expensive brands, like Sony, Gucci, and Rolex. After all, there's no point in trying to peddle cheap stuff.

There's an important lesson here. The more valuable a virtue is to real Christianity and the more clearly it showcases the glory of the image of God in Jesus, the more likely Satan is to copy it. Humility is a precious thing, which is why Satan loves imitating it. And though you cannot truly copy humility, Satan does his best. He's constantly trying to create counterfeits to deceive as many people as possible.

Satan counterfeits humility in two ways. The first way is by crushing people under the weight of circumstances or sin. This is what we see in people whose lives unravel because of a personal tragedy. They're overwhelmed by circumstances and confront the fact that they're not in control of things. Instead, they realize they're small, powerless, and weak. It can also happen when a person's life unravels because of their own sin. They make a poor decision, and everything falls apart in a relationship with a spouse or a parent. And they feel, rightly so, overwhelmed with grief and sorrow.

These kinds of experiences can create a humble-looking demeanor. They can get people going to church, reading their Bible, and talking to their pastor. And God often uses these circumstances to refine genuine faith. But if the real thing isn't already there, it won't produce the fruit of humility. It will lead to what the apostle Paul calls "worldly grief" (2 Corinthians 7:10) — a sense of remorse over circumstances or sin that fails to lead to growth in faith and godly character.

Real humility, on the other hand, is what Paul calls "godly grief." And what makes it godly grief is that it leads to repentance — a turning away from sin and to Christ in faith. Worldly grief won't produce repentance. It may produce some moral reform, but it's temporary, not permanent. The person will not be changed in a way that leads to more dependence on Christ or love for God. Worldly grief, as Paul says, goes nowhere — it only produces death.

Those who are "religious" can suffer from an even more subtle form of false humility. If you look at the billions of people who practice one of the major world religions, you will often find this kind of false humility. It is an appearance of humility that comes from self-denial — when you forgo a physical comfort or a personal privilege. Sometimes we call this asceticism, a self-denying way of life, and it is often regarded as real humility. Sadly, it is nothing but a sophisticated counterfeit.

Christians are particularly susceptible to confusing false humility for the real thing. The believers in Colossae seem to have embraced a kind of asceticism that Paul calls "false humility" (Colossians 2:18 NIV). They were submitting themselves to stringent restrictions in matters of food and drink, as well as practices of worship. But as Paul says, this severity to the body, while appearing wise and humble, is only "promoting self-made religion," which has "no value in stopping the indulgence of the flesh" (Colossians 2:23).

We also find this "false humility" with the Pharisees in Jesus' day. When they fasted, they looked gloomy, engaging in heroic acts of self-denial to impress the less committed. But Jesus sees right through this veneer of humility to the heart of their self-righteousness. And so Jesus advised his followers not to avoid fasting or other spiritual disciplines, but to practice them in a way that doesn't draw any attention to oneself (Matthew 6:16–18).

TAKING STEPS TOWARD HUMILITY

We live in a culture that is hostile to humility. Our entire economic system, free-market capitalism, runs on the principle of competition—getting ahead and beating the other guy. Politics is often predicated on asserting one's rights, usually over against other people. And as a culture, we're increasingly characterized by fear and self-protection, which tends to put roadblocks in the way of loving others as we would want to be loved. Ours is a society that specializes in self-promotion. Pursue the American Dream! Put yourself first! None of this will help you learn to put to death selfish ambition or vain conceit.

In this culture of pride and ambition, God tells us to not think of ourselves more highly than we ought (Romans 12:3). Jesus puts it this way: "Whoever humbles himself like this child is the greatest in the kingdom of heaven" (Matthew

18:4). The prophet Zephaniah cries out, "Seek humility" (Zephaniah 2:3). From the apostle Peter the charge comes: "Humble yourselves" (1 Peter 5:6). And James, the brother of Jesus, reminds us, "God opposes the proud, but gives grace to the humble" (James 4:6). Paul simply says we ought to put on humility (Colossians 3:12).

If only it were that easy—like putting on a winter coat! Unfortunately, it's not. But that doesn't mean we should give up. It doesn't mean we are passive in this process. There are things we can do to make genuine strides to move in a humble direction. But we need to begin in a counterintuitive place. We must first admit and confess that humble we're not. "'Tis inexpressible, and almost inconceivable," observed Jonathan Edwards, "how strong a self-righteous, self-exalting disposition is naturally in man; and what he will not do and suffer, to feed and gratify it."[20]

This is precisely why C. S. Lewis offered this simple yet sage advice when pursuing humility: "The first step is to realize that one is proud." Lewis then adds, "If you think you are not conceited, it means you are very conceited indeed."[21]

But confessing our pride or our lack of humility isn't all there is to it. We can also *ask* for humility. This means adding humility to your prayer list. Realize that when you do this, God may do something unexpected in your life to help you grow in humility. He may lead you through the wilderness for a few years, like he did with the Israelites, "that he might humble you, testing you to know what was in your heart" (Deuteronomy 8:2).

Or he may send you "a thorn" in your flesh, as he did Paul, even though Paul pleaded for it to be removed. Paul prayed several times, asking for God to end his suffering, but God didn't take it away. Why not? Paul tells us that it was to help him avoid becoming conceited, to keep him humble and dependent, relying not on his own strength but on Christ's (see 2 Corinthians 12:7–10 NIV).

After praying and asking, there's another step we should consider. Resist the temptation to take credit for the good things in your life. Develop, instead, the habit of recognizing God as the giver of every good and perfect gift. In other words, develop a habit of gratitude, giving thanks for what God has given you. As Paul says, writing to the cocksure Corinthians, "What do you have that you did not receive? If then you received it, why do you boast as if you did not receive it?" (1 Corinthians 4:7).

Many of us, if we are honest, think of ourselves like King Nebuchadnezzar of Babylon, who one day went out on the roof of the royal palace and said, "Is not this great Babylon, which I have built by my mighty power as a royal residence and for the glory of my majesty?" (Daniel 4:30). We may give a hat tip to God, but deep inside we think our success is largely the result of our own blood, sweat, and tears. But the way to humility is to learn to say with King David, "Who am I, O Lord God, and what is my house, that you have brought me thus far?" (2 Samuel 7:18).

If you know you have been saved by the sacrifice of Jesus Christ, and only by his sacrifice on your behalf, then don't take credit for getting saved. "For by grace you have been saved through faith. And this is not your own doing; it is the gift of God, not a result of works, so that no one may boast" (Ephesians 2:8–9). There's no shame in ascribing your salvation entirely to God. Let him get all the credit for providing you the gift of faith so that you could lay hold of his salvation.

Most importantly—don't miss this—if your humility is going to be genuine, it must *flow from faith*. You must treasure God's promises, and let your confidence in his Word fuel your humility. What promise does Scripture give to encourage us to walk humbly before God and others? "Humble yourselves, therefore, under the mighty hand of God," Peter writes, "so that at the proper time he may exalt you" (1 Peter 5:6). Or listen to this remarkable promise from Jesus, one he often repeats: "Whoever exalts himself will be humbled, and whoever humbles himself will be exalted" (Matthew 23:12).

This is where the pursuit of humility is truly counterintuitive: *You should place your hope in your future exaltation.* At first, this sounds proud, but let me assure you, it's entirely biblical! Jesus is not averse to sharing glory with you. Indeed, he plans to exalt you—if you will humble yourself now and meet the needs of others. If you refuse this stunning promise of future exaltation, then you will be humbled to the dust, and below the dust—forever and ever. But if, by faith, you will walk along the path of humility, then you can anticipate "praise and glory and honor at the revelation of Jesus Christ" (1 Peter 1:7).

JOHN STOTT'S THREE RENUNCIATIONS

I admire few Christians more than John Stott. Evidently, I'm not alone in my esteem for this remarkable individual. In 2005, *Time* magazine named Stott one of the 100 most influential people in the world—alongside Bill Clinton, Barack Obama, Steve Jobs, Bill Gates, Nelson Mandela, and Oprah Winfrey. Not bad for a soft-spoken, celibate Anglican cleric.

John Stott was a powerful communicator and a sharp thinker, who had a legendary work ethic—the stuff that makes for megalomaniacs, not gracious servants of Jesus. And yet, having met Stott, having heard him preach, and having talked with his closest colleagues, it's clear he was a humble man.

Stott's humility wasn't cheap. Humility always has a cost to it, and his cost him dearly. Stott would refer to his "three renunciations"—three momentous decisions he made to not cling to privilege or position so that he could better love God and others. The first was when he decided to forgo an academic post; the second was when he let go of the prospect of getting married; and the third was when he declined the opportunity to become a bishop in the Church of England.[22]

John Stott exemplified humility. He didn't grasp, as we so often do, for what might have been—the satisfaction of an academic career, the intimacy of marriage, the prestige of a bishopric. Instead, these he set aside for the sake of others, from all walks of life and nearly every corner of the globe— North and South America, Europe, Africa, Asia. Following in the footsteps of his Master, he counted others more significant than himself.

In June 2012, John Stott died at the age of ninety, leaving behind an impressive array of books authored, ministries founded, lives impacted, and organizations led. Now he awaits his final exaltation, having learned to humble himself under God's mighty hand so that at the proper time God may exalt him (1 Peter 5:6).

LEARN FROM HIM WHO IS LOWLY IN HEART

Each one of us has people in our lives we are called to love, both for their good and for Jesus' sake. Yet we must admit that we fall short of loving them as we ought because of our pride, our lack of humility. We're too interested in asking the questions Simon the Pharisee asked: *Who and what sort of person is this? What have they done to deserve my help?* Rather than following the path of Jesus, who counted the needs of others more significant than his own, we hang on to our privileges or prerogatives.

But when we are humbled and our hearts are freed to love others without regard to their status or position, everything changes. Our mind-set shifts, and the way is cleared for love to flow from our lives into the lives of others in a way that honors Christ.

Jesus invites us to learn the way of humility by drawing near to him: "Come to me, all who labor and are heavy laden, and I will give you rest. Take my yoke upon you, and learn from me, for I am gentle and lowly in heart, and you will find rest for your souls" (Matthew 11:28–29). And as we do, we will find ourselves becoming even a bit more humble—"delightedly humble, feeling the infinite relief of having for once got rid of all the silly nonsense about your own dignity which has made you restless and unhappy all your life."[23]

CHAPTER RESOURCES

QUESTIONS FOR REFLECTION

1. Before reading this chapter, how would you have defined humility? How has your view of humility changed by reading this chapter?

2. What misconceptions of humility do you see prevalent in your relationships?

3. What are the signs of humility you have seen in the lives of others? How is that an encouragement to you?

4. The antithesis to humility is pride, and sometimes it can be dressed up to look like humility. Read Luke 7:36 – 39, especially verse 39. How is pride dressed up in this situation? Where have you seen this or participated in it yourself?

5. Read Colossians 2:18 – 22. How can the false humility of submitting to restrictions lead to pride? Where have you seen this or participated in it yourself?

6. This chapter lists several steps that are helpful in putting on true humility. Read through the list and identify the steps you need to take to grow in humility.

SCRIPTURES TO PONDER

- Proverbs
- Daniel 4 – 5
- 1 Corinthians 3 – 4
- Philippians 2 – 3
- James 4

BOOKS TO HELP YOU DIG DEEPER

Dickson, John. *Humilitas: A Lost Key to Life, Love, and Leadership*. Grand Rapids: Zondervan, 2011.

Keller, Tim. *The Freedom of Self-Forgetfulness: The Path to True Christian Joy*. Chorley, UK: 10Publishing, 2012.

Mahaney, C. J. *Humility: True Greatness*. Sisters, OR: Multnomah, 2005.

Murray, Andrew. *Humility*. Kensington, PA: Whitaker House, 2005.

Biographies for Encouragement

Cameron, Julia. *John Stott: The Humble Leader*. Fearn, Ross-shire, Scotland: Christian Focus, 2012.

Tada, Joni Eareckson. *The God I Love: A Lifetime of Walking with Jesus*. Grand Rapids: Zondervan, 2003.

4

MEEKNESS: A LAMBLIKE DISPOSITION

On July 8, 1838, the seventh president of the United States, General Andrew Jackson, informed his minister, the Reverend Dr. John Edgar, that he wanted to become a member of the Presbyterian Church and receive Communion. Dr. Edgar asked the president about his conversion and convictions, and gave his approving nod with each satisfactory answer.

But Dr. Edgar was a godly minister, and he felt the need to probe the president's soul more deeply. "General, there is one more question which it is my duty to ask you," he announced. "Can you forgive all your enemies?"

The question stunned General Jackson. He stared at his minister for a moment while he gathered his thoughts. He then broke the silence: "My political enemies, I can freely forgive," Jackson confessed. "But as for those who abused me when I was serving my country in the field, and those who attacked me for serving my country—Doctor, that is a different case."

This was an honest answer, but Dr. Edgar wasn't satisfied. Christians must forgive all, he insisted to America's seventh president. This was absolute.[24]

Unlike Andrew Jackson, few of us have had to suffer in the service of our country. But each of us knows how hard it is to forgive—to bear injury from others, from those who have mistreated us.

And yet Dr. Edgar was correct in his insistence that Christians must forgive *all*. Followers of Jesus will suffer mistreatment with *a lamblike disposition*—the kind we see in Jesus.[25] Slights and slanders, hurts and harms are met with meekness, not hostility.

This, biblically speaking, is not optional. Forgiving others is one of the defining marks of a real Christian.

BLESSED ARE THE MEEK

We find a compelling picture of what it means to be real in this way in Jesus' famous Sermon on the Mount. Jesus begins with a series of blessings we have come to call the Beatitudes: "Blessed are the poor in spirit, for theirs is the kingdom of heaven. Blessed are those who mourn, for they shall be comforted. Blessed are the meek, for they shall inherit the earth," and so on (Matthew 5:3–5).

We should pay attention to Jesus' audience—the ones he declares these blessings to. He is speaking to *followers who face the reality of suffering and persecution.* "Blessed are those who are persecuted for righteousness' sake," Jesus says, "for theirs is the kingdom of heaven. Blessed are you when others revile you and persecute you and utter all kinds of evil against you falsely on my account" (Matthew 5:10–11). Jesus wants to galvanize the souls of his disciples, readying them to meet injury from others with lamblike grace.

Authentic Christians reflect Christ's character in many different ways—from their love of truth to their pursuit of justice. But there's something singularly powerful about the quality we sometimes call meekness, this forgiving disposition. According to Jonathan Edwards, meekness possesses and governs their lives—"it is their true and proper character."[26]

THE POWER OF MEEKNESS

Meekness isn't a word we often use today, even in Christian circles. And admittedly, it's not a very appealing word. It doesn't suggest inspiring images—we don't think of a brave soldier or a courageous leader or a champion athlete. Instead, we see doormats, mousy people who let other people walk all over them.

But meekness isn't weakness. It's an expression of strength, a quality of character that is rooted in profound confidence and self-composure. Meekness produces serenity of mind, repose of soul, quietness of heart, even amidst criticism or ill-treatment. It's a sign, not of weakness, but of power, the likes of which we seldom see in our competitive, tit-for-tat, road-rage world.

Meekness reveals an inner power of mind and heart that enables a person to bear injury without being emotionally turned upside down or inside out. Jonathan Edwards uses the image of a large, coursing river to describe how meekness expands and even strengthens the soul so that it is unperturbed by the wrongs we suffer. He writes:

> It is from littleness of soul that the mind is easily disturbed and put out of frame by the reproaches and the ill treatment of men; as we see that little streams of waters are much disturbed in their course by small unevennesses and obstacles that they meet with, and make a great deal of noise as they pass over them, whereas great and mighty streams would pass over them calmly and quietly, smooth and unruffled.[27]

Linger on this image for a moment. Imagine you've been snubbed or spoken against or sidelined in some way. Yet you choose not to respond with a whipped-up, indignant froth on the inside. Can you envision having this type of self-control? If so, it is the result of God's gracious gift of meekness in you, enlarging your heart so that you are no longer disquieted by the rocks of injury or the tiny pebbles of criticism that come your way. Instead, like the Mississippi, you're unchanged by these slight offenses. Mighty and majestic, you keep rolling on, "calmly and quietly, smooth and unruffled."

Proverbs describes the strength of meekness when it says, "Whoever is slow to anger is better than the mighty, and he who rules his spirit than he who takes a city" (16:32). The apostle Paul reminds us that meekness flows from love, and he tells us what it looks like in action—it's "not irritable or resentful" (1 Corinthians 13:5).

Or think of Moses, who, the book of Numbers tells us, "was very meek, more than all people who were on the face of the earth" (12:3). It's a good thing too, because the children of Israel bellyached constantly to Moses. They complained nonstop about his leadership, even to the point of criticizing his character. During those forty years of tedious wilderness wanderings, how many countless injuries did Moses endure from his own feckless flock?

TWO EXTREMES AND ONE COUNTERFEIT

How we respond to injuries from others is the acid test of our authenticity. We know whether we're real by how our hearts respond when we are hurt, insulted, falsely accused, or confronted with something we'd rather not hear about ourselves. Are we combative, quick to want to throw a counterpunch? Or are we gracious, ready to absorb the hurt, knowing Jesus has already suffered it all?

Scripture furnishes us with a myriad of examples of meekness — and its opposites. Consider a man named Abishai, one of King David's loyal followers. David and his entourage enter a small village in Israel, and there a man begins to curse David, throwing stones at him and accusing him of being a worthless bum. Abishai hears this offensive nonsense and says indignantly to David, "Why should this dead dog curse my lord the king? Let me go over and take off his head" (2 Samuel 16:9). Needless to say, that's *not* meekness.

On the other hand, we can tend toward the opposite extreme, not of aggressiveness, but of passivity. We can pretend we are being meek when all we're doing is dodging conflict to please people or save face. That's not meekness; that's mousiness — and it's certainly not honest or real. We don't arrive at meekness by combining passivity and aggressiveness to become *passive-aggressive* either. In fact, that's meekness's biggest counterfeit. We see passive-aggressive behavior in willful people who know they can't be all "in your face," but who lack the spiritual wherewithal to have true meekness. Inside, the wolf is alive and well, but they don the gentle demeanor of a lamb to avoid scaring anyone. They modulate their voice, force a smile, and play the part of Mr. or Mrs. Congeniality, even though they're a hissing cauldron of pride, bitterness, and animosity. In my experience, these folks are the most vexing in a church, because they're not honest with themselves, or with others, about what's going on in their souls — even though everyone around them sees the aggression they are desperately trying to hide.

JESUS CHRIST, THE LAMB OF GOD

If we want a truly convincing picture of meekness, we must look to Jesus Christ. Much is said about Jesus in the four gospels. But nothing is emphasized more consistently than his loving response to injury from others; nothing is stressed more than his lamblike disposition toward his enemies and adversaries.

There is a reason that Jesus is called the Lamb of God. It's not only because of *what* he does — "Behold, the Lamb of God, who takes away the sin of the world!" (John 1:29). It is also because of *how* he does it — "*Like a sheep* he was led to the slaughter and *like a lamb* before its shearers is silent, so he opens not his mouth" (Acts 8:32, emphasis added). Like a sheep, like a lamb, silent and sacrificial in the face of opponents. That's meekness.

Lambs aren't aggressive. They're not pugnacious or rowdy. They don't eat their young or threaten their owners.

They are gentle creatures. So, too, is the Lamb of God, Jesus Christ, even amidst insults and injuries from friends and enemies alike.

Jesus was a lamb led to the slaughter. He was misunderstood by the masses. He was disowned by his family. He was demonized by religious leaders. He was betrayed by a close associate. He was abandoned by his most intimate followers. He was cursed in a court of law. He was belittled by a "big man" who presumed to play his judge. He was mocked mercilessly by ignorant soldiers. He was insulted by a crucified criminal. He was rejected by the crowds.

But how does the Lamb of God respond? With hostility, vindictiveness, and offense? Does he upbraid Pontius Pilate, or call down lightning on Judas? Does he invoke omniscience to undermine his accusers, or summon an archangel to argue his case? What do we see of the God-man in his hour of greatest need? How do absolute strength and authority reveal themselves in the Son of Man? Jonathan Edwards again says it well:

> Not in the exercise of any fiery passions; not in fierce and violent speeches, and vehemently declaiming against, and crying out of the intolerable wickedness of opposers, giving 'em their own in plain terms; but in not opening his mouth when afflicted and oppressed, in going as a lamb to the slaughter, and as a sheep before his shearers, is dumb, not opening his mouth; praying that the Father would forgive his cruel enemies, because they knew not what they did; not shedding others' blood; but with all-conquering patience and love, shedding his own.[28]

"All-conquering patience and love" — that's a perfect definition of biblical meekness.

FOLLOWING IN THE FOOTSTEPS OF THE LAMB

If we're real, we will look something like Jesus, the Lamb of God. Our lives will be defined by the same disposition we see in him. We will be marked by meekness, a posture of forgiveness, a willingness to suffer wrongs. But what will this look like in our lives?

Being meek means we respond to resistance or rejection with patience rather than anger or retaliation. When we lack the meekness of Christ, we're incensed if people don't do things our way. In Luke's gospel we're told of a time when two of Jesus' closest followers, James and John, lost their cool when they were rejected by residents of a village in Samaria. Rather than bearing this affront with meekness, they asked Jesus if they should incinerate the place. "Lord, do you want us to tell fire to come down from heaven and consume them?" (Luke 9:54). Not exactly what we'd call meek.

Meekness also receives criticism or rebuke with an eagerness to learn from it rather than to reject it out of hand. Proud people won't tolerate criticism of any kind, much less face-to-face rebuke, even when it's offered in love. That's why the Bible says that the proud are fools; they have no capacity to learn from those around them — even from God himself. "A wise son hears his father's instruction, but a scoffer does not listen to rebuke" (Proverbs 13:1). Meek people, on the other hand, are ready to embrace criticism or receive rebuke, even when the criticism is off the mark, or the rebuke short of love. "A rebuke goes deeper into a man of understanding than a hundred blows into a fool" (Proverbs 17:10).

Meekness also responds to accusations with serene silence

rather than with loud protest. In this we are called to follow in the footsteps of the Lamb of God, as the apostle Peter reminds us:

> For what credit is it if, when you sin and are beaten for it, you endure? But if when you do good and suffer for it you endure, this is a gracious thing in the sight of God. For to this you have been called, because Christ also suffered for you, leaving you an example, so that you might follow in his steps. He committed no sin, neither was deceit found in his mouth. When he was reviled, he did not revile in return; when he suffered, he did not threaten, but continued entrusting himself to him who judges justly.
>
> 1 Peter 2:20–23

Meekness responds to enemies with forgiveness rather than with vengeance. This is where the rubber of meekness meets the road of real life. And this is where the intersection of these two is often messy and painful. Yet this is what we see in our Lord's example as he hung from the cross: "Father, forgive them, for they know not what they do" (Luke 23:34). This same example we see in Stephen as an enraged mob hurled stones at him: "And falling to his knees he cried out with a loud voice, 'Lord, do not hold this sin against them'" (Acts 7:60).

This means retaliation is out of the question, as is revenge — what the Bible calls repaying evil for evil: "Repay no one evil for evil, but give thought to do what is honorable in the sight of all" (Romans 12:17). So, too, is harboring grudges or boiling in bitterness for days, weeks, or even months. This is why

Jesus threatens such serious consequences for being unforgiving: "So also my heavenly Father will do to every one of you, if you do not forgive your brother from your heart" (Matthew 18:35). This isn't optional. If you are real, you will forgive.

ENTRUST YOURSELF TO HIM WHO JUDGES JUSTLY

How we deal with wrongs inflicted on us, how we respond to the hurts that others commit against us—all of this reveals our heart. And though it is painful, it is also helpful in refining our faith and renewing our character in the likeness of Christ. You'll know, then, you're not where you should be—that meekness is a struggle for you, or even a stranger to you—if you find yourself harboring bitterness toward others, are quick to get angry when wronged, find yourself easily agitated and annoyed when slighted, or relish the prospect of revenge against those who have mistreated you.

But how do you attain this lamblike disposition? Where does meekness come from? To become meek you must *entrust yourself to the sovereign goodness of God*. If you're going to be lamblike in the face of injuries, you must believe God's sovereign hand superintends everything that happens to you.

Do you recall what Scripture says about God's role in that greatest of all injuries—the crucifixion of his own Son? Jesus was "delivered up according to the definite plan and foreknowledge of God" (Acts 2:23). God not only foreknew his Son's death; he foreordained it. It wasn't an accident, an unforeseen travesty of justice that God tried to prevent but couldn't. No, it was Plan A from God's perspective.

And so when the apostles are released from prison, they lifted up their voices in prayer and acknowledged the Lord as sovereign, saying that Herod, Pontius Pilate, the Gentiles, and the people of Israel did to Jesus "whatever your hand and your plan had predestined to take place" (Acts 4:28).

Linger on the implications of this astonishing statement for a moment. Set this book down if necessary and really let it sink in. God ordained every demeaning word that belittled Jesus' infinite worth, every ounce of spit that struck his holy face, every drop of blood that flowed from his open wounds. So, too, a gracious yet mysterious God ordains whatsoever comes to pass in your life, even the painful stuff.

No one endured greater injury than Jesus. Yet no one exhibited greater meekness than him. But what was the well-spring from which his meekness flowed? The apostle Peter explains: "When he was reviled, he did not revile in return; when he suffered, he did not threaten, *but continued entrusting himself to him who judges justly*" (1 Peter 2:23, emphasis added). Jesus held unswervingly to his confidence in the just judgment of God the Father. That was the key to sustaining a lamblike disposition in the face of horrific treatment and opposition. If you don't believe in the judgment of God, you will have a difficult time meekly bearing mistreatment.

To become meek you must also remember *God's meekness toward you.* It is the meekness of God that explains why you're still alive—why any one of us is still alive. Imagine how incensed you can be when someone wrongs you, criticizes your actions, judges your motives, or impugns your character. Now, just imagine how an infinitely holy and perfectly good God must feel as he endures countless millions of insults and injuries to his character each day. If we were God, we would have used our omnipotence to incinerate the world long ago! And yet God's meekness leaves open the door of salvation for even the worst of sinners, the vilest of offenders (see Romans 2:4).

MEEKNESS TRIUMPHS

Ultimately, as with all the marks we are looking at, to become meek you must have the life of Christ living within you. Jesus invites us to come to him and learn from him: "Come to me, all who labor and are heavy laden," Jesus says, "and I will give you rest. Take my yoke upon you, and learn from me, for I am gentle and lowly in heart, and you will find rest for your souls" (Matthew 11:28–29).

Meekness is what President Andrew Jackson needed on the day he was admitted into the Presbyterian Church. Asked to forgive his enemies, he came to see that a lamblike disposition, this necessity to forgive those who have wronged us, is one of the essential marks of a real Christian.

President Jackson wasn't anticipating that he would be probed and questioned in this way by Dr. Edgar. And yet when the time came for him to respond, he knew he had to embrace the claim of the gospel on his life. Jackson's biographer gives us his response:

> The stricken man sighed. There was a "considerable pause." Then Jackson spoke again. Upon reflection, he began, he thought he could forgive all who had injured him, even those who reviled him for his services to his country on the battlefield. He was at long last prepared to grant amnesty to all the scoundrels and poltroons who had ever crossed his path.[29]

On July 15, 1838, General Andrew Jackson, seventh president of the United States, was admitted into the Presbyterian Church. He was seventy years old when his battle-weathered soul and tired body knelt to receive Communion for the first time. And as he did, his biographer tells us, "tears of penitence and joy trickled down his careworn cheeks."[30]

Meekness had triumphed.

CHAPTER RESOURCES

QUESTIONS FOR REFLECTION

1. A central theme in the Beatitudes described in Matthew 5:1 – 12, and displayed in the life of Jesus, is meekness (see Philippians 2:3 – 8). What are signs of meekness you have seen in the lives of others?

2. What are misconceptions to meekness that are prevalent in your relationships to others?

3. Why is meekness so central to being a real, authentic Christian?

4. This chapter lists various responses that display meekness. Read through them again, and discuss with a friend the response in which you want to experience better growth.

5. In Matthew 18:21 – 35, Jesus describes unforgiveness in serious terms. Why is this? And how does this relate to meekness?

6. Why is trusting in the sovereignty of God essential to meekness? Consider a time when you were wronged and felt bitter about it. How might trusting in God's sovereignty have helped you respond with greater meekness?

SCRIPTURES TO PONDER

- Numbers 12
- Mark 14 – 15
- Acts 7:54 – 60
- 1 Peter 2:17 – 25

BOOKS TO HELP YOU DIG DEEPER

Jones, L. Gregory. *Embodying Forgiveness: A Theological Analysis*. Grand Rapids: Eerdmans, 1995.

Lane, Timothy S., and Paul David Tripp. *Relationships: A Mess Worth Making*. Greensboro, SC: New Growth, 2008.

Lewis, C. S. "On Forgiveness," in *The Weight of Glory: And Other Addresses*. 1976. Reprint, New York: HarperCollins, 2001.

Yancey, Philip. *What's So Amazing About Grace?* Grand Rapids: Zondervan, 1997.

Biographies for Encouragement

Hopkins, Hugh Evan. *Charles Simeon of Cambridge*. Grand Rapids: Eerdmans, 1977.

Saint, Steve. *End of the Spear: A True Story*. Carol Stream, IL: Tyndale, 2005.

5

CONTRITION: THE GOSPEL EMOTION

Bob was a student I met while I was teaching a course on New Testament theology at a college in Southern California. But Bob wasn't your typical student. He was far older than the rest of his class of twentysomethings. Bob was eighty-four. But even more than just the fact of his age, Bob had a very different story to tell.

Bob was a career military man, and he had fought in three different wars—World War II, the Korean War, and the Vietnam War. His mother had died when he was just twelve, leaving him to be raised by his aunt and uncle. When Bob turned eighteen, he was turned out of their house and had to fend for himself. To complicate things even further, Bob has had a lifelong struggle with same-sex attraction.

Bob didn't meet Jesus until the ripe old age of seventy-nine. He was led to Christ by a young man in his early twenties, a lifeguard at the YMCA where he exercised. And now Bob is a new creation—redeemed through and through. He has become real by the power of God. What you now see in Bob's life is a profound mix of *grief* as he recalls his former way of life and *gratitude* because of the undeserved mercy he has found in the gospel.

Bob always sat in the front row of the class and listened intently to every word that was said. He often wanted to interject something into the discussion, but couldn't compose himself quickly enough to get the words out. He was too overwhelmed with emotion. So he would just clasp his hands together, raise them in a cheering motion, and register his approval by letting out a whimper or groan as he held back tears of joy.

Toward the end of the week, I sat down with Bob and listened to him recount his story of grace. He often had to stop and gasp for air because the realization that Christ's undeserved mercy had invaded his life of sin took his breath away. The swells of emotion made him weep. And his response caused me to weep as well, more than once. I said to Bob at one point, "Bob, all I know is I want to be near you when you see Jesus for the first time face-to-face." He smiled at the thought.

When Bob reflects on over three-quarters of a century of life apart from Christ, he is overcome with regret, and sorrow and sadness wash over him. And yet Bob now understands a profound truth: There is something God will not despise — *a broken and contrite heart*. Contrition is another mark of authentic faith.

A BROKEN AND CONTRITE HEART

Contrition is brokenheartedness over sin. It is how real Christians respond to sin in their lives, while a lack of contrition shows us that a person isn't real. If you're real, you will have experienced contrition, and you will go on experiencing it. You will have firsthand experience with the "broken and contrite heart" of which David speaks (Psalm 51:17).

Everyone responds to sin in some way, whether they call it sin or not. God has hardwired human beings to react to sin. We feel shame or embarrassment or the fear of punishment or regret or guilt. All of these are natural responses to the reality of sin, but *none of them* are what the Bible calls contrition.

Contrition is a uniquely Christian response to sin — it is a gospel response, indeed, *a gospel emotion.*[31] Contrition happens in your heart when you see your sin in light of God's mercy. To be contrite is to experience both sorrow and joy simultaneously — grief because of the depravity of your heart, yet joy because of the prospect of God's grace.

Contrition means owning up to the painful fact that you fall short of the glory of God and are without excuse (see Romans 3:23), yet embracing the joyful news that God has given us the free gift of eternal life in Christ Jesus our Lord (see Romans 6:23). Thus, contrition mirrors the paradox of the gospel as a paradoxical emotion — a pleasing pain, a glad grief, a beautiful brokenness, a weeping over who you are, even as you rejoice over who Christ is for you.

COUNTERFEITS OF CONTRITION

There are other responses to sin, some that look similar to contrition. We easily confuse these with contrition and assume they are evidence that we are real, that we have been born again. But each of these responses is common to both

Christians and non-Christians alike; there's nothing distinctively Christian about them.

Consider, for example, the *fear of punishment*. Every parent knows that the prospect of punishment can elicit strong reaction in a child, whether in the form of a time-out, spanking, or loss of some privilege. And yet underneath these expressions of disappointment, tears, and sadness, there may be little, if any, fear of *wrongdoing itself*—only a desire to avoid the unpleasant consequences of wrongdoing. Contrition is not a fear of punishment; it is a fear of *displeasing the one who ought to be obeyed*.

Or consider another response to sin I'm sure we are all quite familiar with—*regret*. To regret something is to wish you hadn't done it because you now see the impact it's had on you or someone else. You regret losing your cool with your kids because it made your four-year-old cry, or you regret not calling home when away on business because it left your spouse feeling worried. Most of the time, people regret the consequences—they wish they had not happened. But contrition is truly regretting the action itself—quite apart from its impact on anyone else. More than that, it's regretting the one who did it—namely, *yourself*. Contrition makes you the object of your own regret, which is why it penetrates so deeply and hurts so profoundly. You own your actions, acknowledge they're wrong, and regret that you're the kind of person who does such things.

There's yet another common reaction to sin, which we call *embarrassment*. This is what we feel when we are seen in a negative light. Embarrassment works off of our pride and vanity, our love of self and reputation. As such it can be a powerful motivation; the prospect of someone finding out that I did something is often enough to keep me from doing it. As a church staff, we use Covenant Eyes filtering software, and the thought of a colleague finding out that I'd looked at pornography is painful enough in itself to keep me from doing it. But that's not the same as being moved by contrition — an aversion to the sin itself.

Guilt is a fourth common response to sin; it's also the one most easily confused with contrition. But there's a world of difference between the two. Using theological terms, we might say that while contrition is a gospel emotion, guilt is a *law emotion*. For guilt is what you feel when you know you've violated a standard or fallen short of an ideal. God uses guilt, of course, to draw people to himself, indeed to drive them to Christ. But the feeling of guilt itself isn't a uniquely Christian response to sin.

Now, by calling these counterfeits of contrition, I don't mean to imply that these are illegitimate reactions to sin. There's obviously a place for embarrassment or fear of punishment or regret or guilt. It's not that these are inappropriate responses to sin; in fact, each has a helpful, if subordinate, part to play in curbing sin in our life. Yet none of these are what the Bible calls contrition.

"MY SIN IS EVER BEFORE ME"

Nowhere do we find contrition better exemplified than in Psalm 51. The penitent king David penned this prayer in the aftermath of his colossal sin with Bathsheba. God sent the prophet Nathan to confront David, and David no doubt responded the same way we would if we were confronted as the perpetrator of a heinous crime—with shame, guilt, remorse, and fear of punishment (see 2 Samuel 12:1–15).

Yet somewhere along the way, brokenness and grace came together in David's soul, and he found himself experiencing contrition. Psalm 51 represents David's effort to put his experience to words; it provides us with the language, even the lyric, of contrition.[32]

And what does David's contrite heart now understand about his sin? First, David sees the *pervasiveness* of his sin. You won't arrive at a place of contrition until you realize sin is everywhere. It's in your soul and in your life, it's everywhere you turn, everywhere you go. Contrition won't be a reality for you until you can say with David, "For I know my transgressions, and my sin is *ever before me*" (Psalm 51:3, emphasis added).

Understanding the pervasiveness of sin, whether in society or in your own soul, is a prerequisite to experiencing contrition. Perhaps this is why contrition is so hard to come by these days. For an understanding of the pervasiveness of sin has all but disappeared in our culture. It's not that people sin less today than they did in previous generations. Rather, it's that we as a society no longer use the word *sin* for much of anything—other than a sumptuous piece of chocolate cake on the dessert menu.

Because of the ingenious devilry of modern society, we've invented a thousand ways to talk about the bad things we do without ever having to mention the dreaded "s-word." Nowadays we're prepared to label bad behavior a thousand things—criminal, unhealthy, self-destructive, intolerant, politically incorrect, dysfunctional, but *not* sinful.[33]

Why do terms matter here? Because contrary to popular opinion, sin isn't simply transgression, or the sinful things we do; it also has to do with corruption—with the sinful *people* we are. And thus sin, understood as sinful corruption, is ever present with us in this life. Wherever we go, whatever we do, sin is right there with us. Or as the apostle Paul lamented, "When I want to do right, evil lies close at hand" (Romans 7:21).

Clearly, sin isn't surface deep. If that's how we see it, we'll be deceived about ourselves. And we will fail to experience contrition. David saw things quite differently. His sin with Bathsheba taught him the depth of sin. "Behold, I was brought forth in iniquity, and in sin did my mother conceive me" (Psalm 51:5). Ultimately, David doesn't transfer the blame for his sin to someone else, nor does he look for an alibi in his background or an excuse in his circumstances. Instead, he owns his junk, wholly and completely.

David recognizes that the root of the problem is himself. He is his own worst enemy. That's what a contrite heart owns—that my problem isn't this or that particular sin, but the fact that I'm a sinner to the core. Until you can say with David, "My sin is ever before me," you'll never know "a broken and contrite heart" (Psalm 51:3, 17).

"AGAINST YOU ONLY HAVE I SINNED"

A contrite heart grasps not only sin's pervasiveness but also its offensiveness. When David took Bathsheba, he sinned against many — Bathsheba herself, of course, but also Uriah, her husband; the men David enlisted to help conceal his crime; even the people of Israel who entrusted David with the kingship. And yet notice who David believes has suffered the ultimate offense of his sin. "Against you, you only," he confesses to God, "have I sinned and done what is evil in your sight" (Psalm 51:4).

Gallup reports that among self-identifying born-again Christians, only 17 percent define sin in relationship to God.[34] We live in a therapeutic age in which the real offense of sin — if anything is even identifiable as sin anymore — is that it's not good for you. We shouldn't do bad things because they're not healthy for us. It's not good to get angry or steal or lie or talk behind someone's back or overeat at most meals or sleep with someone else's spouse, because none of these will help promote your best life now!

But the contrite heart knows that sin is first and foremost against God — his law, reputation, character. While there's a horizontal, person-to-person dimension to most sin, it's the vertical, Godward dimension that is fundamental. This is because God is more fundamental, indeed, infinitely more so, than we are. A contrite heart gets this — that every sin is at root a sin against God, and that this is the true heinousness of sin.

SOMETHING WORSE THAN ADULTERY OR MURDER

Yet despite sin's offense, there is still, biblically speaking, a design to it. Of course, a holy God despises sin. In his mysterious providence, however, God uses our sin to promote his purposes, not only in the world, but in our lives as well.

David grasps this stunning truth. From a place of contrition, David can see God's loving design in the tragedy of his own sin, and astonishingly, David appreciates God's loving purpose in that design. He can acknowledge a sovereign rationale behind his tragic mistake. "Behold, you delight in truth in the inward being," he confesses to God, "and you teach me wisdom in the secret heart" (Psalm 51:6). David sees that God is teaching him, using his sin to open his eyes, driving truth home.

Egregious though it was, David's perversity was pedagogy. His sin became a tutorial where he learned invaluable truths about who he is and, more importantly, who God is. And God designed it this way. For God, as Psalm 51 declares, delights in truth — indeed, in the *recognition* of truth within our souls. Hence, God is willing to orchestrate colossal failure in our lives, if by so doing he can bring us to the point of contrition.

Here is a shocking truth. From God's perspective, there's something worse than adultery, or betrayal, or murder. The worst thing a person can do is *fail to find the grace of God*. This is the worst predicament anyone could ever be in. Naturally, you might think nothing could be worse than David's crimes; indeed, they were heinous. But if those very sins bring you to a place where you find the mercy of God, then what would otherwise be deadly is not a dead end, but an opening to paradise through the doorway of contrition.

This is why God is not afraid to use our sin to break us, because he knows he can then rebuild us with his mercy. His love is so fierce he will even allow severe things to happen to us so that we can taste the sweetness of his grace. Not only suffering, but even sin is orchestrated by God to bring about good purposes in our lives. For he wants to bring us to the place called contrition, where we say, "Let me hear joy and gladness; let the bones that *you have broken* rejoice" (Psalm 51:8, emphasis added).

I'm often discouraged by my inability to control my tongue. How difficult it is to be "quick to hear, slow to speak" (James 1:19). Frankly, that may be my least favorite verse in the Bible! In fact, I can engage in conversation with that verse in mind and yet, three minutes into the discussion, find my mouth has taken over; then, three minutes later, I can feel that subtle but painful wave of guilt wash over me as I realize, yes, I've done it again.

But I am learning to recognize a purpose to this struggle. As I wrestle with controlling my tongue, I realize what God means when he says, "If anyone does not stumble in what he says, he is a perfect man, able also to bridle his whole body" (James 3:2). More than that, my own sin helps me marvel at the sinless Savior, who never spoke a single sinful word—not one! This sinless Savior died for me, in my place, in order to forgive every careless word uttered—all of which impresses upon my heart the astonishing grace of God.

"HAVE MERCY ON ME, O GOD"

Unlike guilt, contrition isn't a dead end. Contrition sees a way out of guilt. A contrite heart understands there is a remedy for sin. No one has to live with their guilt forever—or their fear of punishment, regret, embarrassment, or shame. The contrite heart sees in all of this an opening called *mercy*.

Paradoxically, then, contrition is marked by *hope*. This is what we hear from David in his opening plea—not a cry of desperation, but a request of hope: "Have mercy on me, O God, according to your steadfast love" (Psalm 51:1).

Jesus once told a parable to illustrate this gospel emotion we call contrition. It was a story about two men—a very devout, religious man, a Pharisee, and a notorious bad boy, a tax collector.

> He also told this parable to some who trusted in themselves that they were righteous, and treated others with contempt: "Two men went up into the temple to pray, one a Pharisee and the other a tax collector. The Pharisee, standing by himself, prayed thus: 'God, I thank you that I am not like other men, extortioners, unjust, adulterers, or even like this tax collector. I fast twice a week; I give tithes of all that I get.' But the tax collector, standing far off, would not even lift up his eyes to heaven, but beat his breast, saying, 'God, be merciful to me, a sinner!'"
>
> Luke 18:9–14

In Jesus' telling of the story, the Pharisee is not experiencing contrition. Sure, he's thankful that God has kept him from doing all sorts of bad stuff. But he's clearly not broken over his sin in a way that shows he has owned it. He doesn't recognize the pervasiveness of his sin, nor does he grasp the full offense of his sin, or the depth of his sin, or the purpose of his sin. He does not see, or perceive a need for, *a remedy for his sin*. The tax collector, on the other hand, knows his need. He knows he has nothing to offer, nothing to defend him, and so he cries out in the same way David does, with the voice of contrition: "God, be merciful to me, a sinner!"

SAVIOR *OF* SIN, OR SAVIOR *FROM* SIN?

Have you ever experienced a broken and contrite heart? Is that your response to the reality of sin in your life? One of the telltale signs of contrition is when you look to Jesus, not as Savior *of* your sin, but as Savior *from* your sin.[35]

Again, listen to how David pleads with the Lord in Psalm 51 (emphasis added): "According to your abundant mercy *blot out* my transgressions" (verse 1). "*Wash me thoroughly* from my iniquity, and *cleanse me* from my sin!" (verse 2). "*Purge me* with hyssop, and I shall be clean; *wash me*, and I shall be whiter than snow" (verse 7). "Hide your face from my sins, and *blot out* all my iniquities" (verse 9). "*Deliver me* from bloodguiltiness, O God, O God of my salvation" (verse 14). A contrite heart wants salvation *from* sin — deliverance, purging, cleansing.

Some professing Christians love Jesus simply because he is Savior of their sin. They comfort themselves with the thought that Jesus shields them from the consequences of their sin, and then go right on fondling sin itself. This isn't contrition; it's hypocrisy — a deceptively cheap "grace" that brings no lasting change.

If you're not real — if you lack a new heart — you may dislike the guilt of sin, but you will have made a place for sin to remain in your heart. Your sin won't strike you as heinous in its own right. You'll happily assume that you have a Savior who lets you avoid the consequences of sin without asking you to forsake sin. This is the height of presumption, a mockery of God's grace (see Galatians 6:7).

Jesus' brother Jude calls people in this delusional state of mind ungodly, because they "pervert the grace of our God into sensuality and deny our only Master and Lord, Jesus Christ" (Jude 4). With their lips they profess Christ, but with their lives they deny him; they turn grace into an occasion for mischief. For them Jesus is nothing more than Savior of their sin. Paul makes a similar point when he says of certain individuals, "They profess to know God, but they deny him by their works" (Titus 1:16). They're the kind of church-goers who have the appearance of godliness, but deny its power (2 Timothy 3:5).

Ask yourself, then, this question: "How would my life change if I knew I would never have to suffer the conse-quences of sin — if I knew I would never get caught, or pun-ished, or embarrassed, or even feel guilty?" Be honest with yourself. Would knowing this turn you into someone radi-cally different from who you are? Would you want to com-mit sin, knowing there would be no consequences to pay? If so, then it's not a contrite heart or a hatred of sin that holds you back; it is the undesirable prospect of shame, guilt, or grief.

Only a contrite person has had a true change of heart. Only a real Christian grieves over sin *because it's sin* rather than because it brings with it shame, embarrassment, guilt, regret, or punishment. And this is why contrition drives moral transformation. A contrite heart shapes Christlike character because it is a *changed heart* — a heart that delights less in sin and more in holiness, one that grieves more intensely over offending God and strives more earnestly to honor him in all things.

NOW NO CONDEMNATION!

When you're real, you know you've been justified freely by God's grace through the death and resurrection of Jesus (see Romans 5:1). There's nothing you can do to detract from, or add to, Christ's perfect sacrifice (see Hebrews 10:12). Becoming real thus puts an end to the fear of punishment, and you can say with confidence, "There is therefore now no condemnation for those who are in Christ Jesus" (Romans 8:1).

But while the fear of punishment decreases, if not altogether ceases, conviction of sin increases. This is another aspect of the paradox of this gospel emotion—as your fear of punishment decreases, your dread of sin and your dislike of it increase. Even though you have solid assurance, you now have a tender conscience. While the fear of hell is removed, the fear of sin is enlarged. You don't dread God's judgment, but you do his fatherly displeasure. You're less easily shaken in your faith, but more easily troubled by your sin. That's the softening of the heart that comes from contrition.

This is why contrition is the doorway to Christ. No one comes to Jesus through guilt, shame, or regret alone. These are prods to move us in the right direction, but they won't ultimately get us to Christ. In fact, while these serve as guardrails for real Christians, keeping them on the path of obedience, they can be prison bars for non-Christians, who mistake them for the marks of authentic faith.

I came to Christ through the door of contrition. As I look

back on the months leading to my conversion, I see clearly how God used my sin to break me. A series of idiotic decisions left me with a mountain of guilt and shame. But these responses only served to till the soil of my heart, to prepare me to receive the word of the gospel. And when it came, by means of a simple gospel presentation on a coffee-stained napkin in the corner booth of a McDonald's just a mile from my house, there was contrition.

Like David, I found myself broken because of my sin, yet rejoicing because of God's promise of forgiveness. And I cried out, "Jesus, Son of David, have mercy on me!" (Mark 10:47).

Contrition came, and I met Christ.

CHAPTER RESOURCES

QUESTIONS FOR REFLECTION

1. This chapter mentions several different ways we respond to sin, including shame, embarrassment, fear of punishment, regret, and guilt. In light of contrition, seeing your own sin in light of God's mercy, why are these responses incomplete? What makes contrition different?

2. Do you agree that sin has all but disappeared in that our society no longer uses the word *sin* for much of anything? (For example, we have lots of ways to describe bad things we do — criminal, unhealthy in attitude, self-destructive, intolerant, politically incorrect, and dysfunctional.) Have you seen this lack of acknowledgment creep into your own life?

3. God demonstrates his "severe mercy" (see Romans 11:32 – 36) in our lives by using our sin for his purposes so that we will come to know his mercy. How have you seen God's severe mercy in your own life?

4. If it's true that a truly contrite heart wants salvation from sin, not salvation of sin, how do you know whether or not you have a contrite heart?

5. What would you become, or what would your life look like, if you knew you would never suffer any consequences of sin?

6. How can other believers encourage you in your cultivation of a contrite heart? Perhaps there is a deeper question: Do you *want* to cultivate a contrite heart?

SCRIPTURES TO PONDER

- Genesis 1 – 11
- Psalm 51
- Lamentations
- Luke 18:9 – 14
- Romans 1 – 4

BOOKS TO HELP YOU DIG DEEPER

Bridges, Jerry. *Respectable Sins: Confronting the Sins We Tolerate*. Colorado Springs: NavPress, 2007.

Gilbert, Greg. *What Is the Gospel?* Wheaton, IL: Crossway, 2010.

Keller, Timothy. *Counterfeit Gods: The Empty Promises of Money, Sex, and Power, and the Only Hope that Matters*. New York: Dutton, 2009.

Plantinga, Cornelius Jr. *Not the Way It's Supposed to Be: A Breviary of Sin*. Grand Rapids: Eerdmans, 1995.

Roberts, Robert C. *Spiritual Emotions: A Psychology of Christian Virtues*. Grand Rapids: Eerdmans, 2007.

Biographies for Encouragement

Aitken, Jonathan. *John Newton: From Disgrace to Amazing Grace*. Wheaton, IL: Crossway, 2007.

Bunyan, John. *Grace Abounding to the Chief of Sinners*. Grand Rapids: Baker, 1978.

Edwards, Jonathan. *The Life and Diary of David Brainerd*. 1949. Reprint, Peabody, MA: Hendrickson, 2006.

6
WHOLENESS: THE FULL IMAGE OF CHRIST

On our way to the U-505 submarine exhibit at Chicago's Museum of Science and Industry, we always pass through a hall lined with fun-house mirrors. While these are never the main attraction, our family enjoys gazing at our own distorted selves for a few minutes. The use of concave and convex angles creates some hilarious reflections — a huge head on a tiny body or gargantuan legs on a shrunken torso. My kids inevitably get a few laughs out of seeing themselves, and especially their daddy, all distorted and misshaped.

We laugh because we know these images aren't real. If they were, it wouldn't be funny; it would be heartbreaking. And we wouldn't chuckle; we'd cry. We often take for granted the beautiful symmetry and proportionality of the body. Only when we see a distortion, like in a fun-house mirror, do we realize that such a body wouldn't be real, but something grotesque and unreal, like what we might find in a horror film or a science-fiction movie.

ALL THE GRACES IN PERFECT HARMONY

There is a similar truth when we consider our spiritual condition. Those who aren't real, who aren't twice-born, might show some growth in one or two of the Christian graces, but they will be deficient in the rest. They're spiritually off-balance, morally lopsided. If you look closely at their lives, they won't reflect the symmetry we find in the person of Christ. Instead, what you will see is something you would find by looking at a fun-house mirror—distorted images of the Savior, not the fullness of his person.

Those who aren't real may love God's justice, but care little for his grace. They may boast of their salvation, but be blasé about God himself. They may claim to enjoy great intimacy with Christ, but have no fear of the Lord. They may be keen to pursue holiness, yet know nothing of spiritual happiness. They may have zeal for the things of God, yet no patience with the ways of God. They may be bold in their crusade for Christ, yet indignant at an affront to their character. They may loudly decry the ills of our world, yet fail to grasp the waywardness of their own heart. They may become incensed with hypocrisy in the church, yet harbor bitterness toward another Christian for months, even years. They may be adept at pointing out the idols in everyone else's life, yet find it difficult to identify a single struggle in their own.

Real Christians, by contrast, reflect Christ's whole image in their lives and character. And remember how balanced Jesus was. His life was filled with a whole range of graces and virtues. He was meek before accusers, yet bold before Pharisees. He was compassionate toward the hurting, yet forthright with the crowds. He was patient with his disciples, yet overturned tables in the temple. He blasted hypocrisy, yet humbly received scourging. He was eaten up with zeal for God, yet would often slip away quietly to pray.

John, the author of Revelation, rightly sees Jesus Christ as both a lion and a lamb—a profound juxtaposition of imagery that points to an even more profound combination of moral excellencies in Jesus' person. Not a single grace is missing; every virtue is fully represented in the person of Christ.[36]

So it is as well for those who are real, who have the whole image of Christ on them. It's not that you will have every grace to the same degree that Christ had them; Jesus was, of course, the perfect God-man, sinless in every respect. And yet every grace you see in Christ, you will see, at least in seed form, in your own life, precisely because the whole person of Christ has taken up residency within you. As Jonathan Edwards observes, "There is grace in Christians answering to grace in Christ ... the same things that belong to Christ's character, belong to theirs."[37]

Real Christians are Christlike; they're whole, balanced people. Just as we see in the life of Christ a beautiful symmetry and proportionality, so we see the same in the lives of real Christians. Because they've received the *whole* Christ, not a part of him, they bear his whole image. They're not lopsided, but well-rounded, morally and spiritually proportional.

Wholeness is one of the marks of a real Christian, because when you're real, you've received not half of Christ but the whole Christ. When you embrace Jesus, you get all of who he is—not 20 percent, or 60 percent, or 80 percent, but 100 percent. No one gets a part of Christ. *You either have him whole, or you don't have him at all.*

That's why real Christians have *the full image of Christ* on them. Every grace that is his is now ours, the fullness of his life within us. Everything we see in him, we will see ever increasingly in us. If we're real, the fullness of his life, every grace he has, will be on us, at least in principle, and eventually in practice.

SINGLE-ISSUE CHRISTIANS?

Real Christians reflect Christ's likeness, not only in their character, but also in their *thinking*. They have the whole image of Christ, not only on their hearts, but also on their minds. There's a symmetry and balance to how they think— that is, what they wrestle with, what they think about, what concerns them.

You've heard, I'm sure, of single-issue voters. But did you know there's such a thing as *single-issue Christians*? These are professing Christians who think there's only one issue that good Christians should care about. Everything else is optional, or at least not important. These folks have found an element of Christian truth, and that's all they ever talk about. They've set up camp on, say, the doctrine of election, or spiritual warfare, or speaking in tongues, or the love of God, and are now amazingly adept at finding that one truth under every rock—and they can't understand why you don't do the same.

If the Christian faith were like the eighty-eight keys on a gorgeous Steinway piano, they would only ever hit a single key, or strike a single note. And while that one note may be important in its own right, it becomes tedious, if not obnoxious, if that's all you ever hear.

Are you a single-issue Christian? Do you care about one element of truth—and that one truth only? If so, you're probably lopsided. Your life fails to reflect the whole image of Christ in how you think and act.

Of course, we ought to prioritize Christian truth and recognize that some biblical teachings are more important than others. But if we're real, we will enjoy the mind of Christ in an increasing way, which means a mind submitted to the fullness of Scripture, or to what Paul calls "the whole counsel of God" (Acts 20:27).

At the end of the day, single-issue Christians are bad readers of the Bible. Because they fixate on only a part of Scripture, they downplay or dispense with the rest. In fact, they so "rightly divide" the word of truth that most of it is left on the cutting-room floor. But real Christians, those with Christlike wholeness, find wisdom in the advice of Charles Spurgeon, who counseled young preachers with this singular thought: "All revealed truth in harmonious proportion must be your theme."[38]

CLIQUISH CHRISTIANS?

Wholeness of character and mind are Christlike qualities. But so, too, is wholeness in our *relationships*. In other words, real Christians aren't tribal. Nor are they cliquish. They don't show favoritism, and they don't associate with only certain types of people, leaving the rest unnoticed. That's a mark of one who does not know Christ.

Some church folks only spend time with other Christians. They don't have much of a heart for those outside the fold. Some only like to be with people they already know—whether Christian or non-Christian, it doesn't matter, as long as they know them. Others only like to be around people who look like them, talk like them, or act like them. Still others only connect with people of their same age, background, or life stage. Sadly, many churches these days thrive on this demographic ghettoization.

But we'll have to look long and hard to find anything like a tribal mentality in Jesus. He was a friend of tax collectors and sinners (Matthew 11:19). He invited children into his midst (Matthew 19:13–15). He healed a demon-possessed man (Mark 5:1–20). He debated with religious scholars (Matthew 22:15–46). He talked with a Samaritan woman (John 4:1–26). And he ate with a repentant rich man named Zacchaeus (Luke 19:1–10).

You see, we can't pigeonhole Jesus, as though he only conversed with or cared about certain types of people. In a sense, his relationships were unpredictable; he interacted with a vast array of persons and personalities. You might say he wasn't given to affinity-based ministry.

How predictable are your relationships? Of course, there isn't anything wrong with enjoying people similar to you. But it is a problem, and reveals a lack of Christlikeness, when you relate *only* or *exclusively* to the same sorts of people.

What Christlikeness calls for, then, is biblical hospitality. But let me hasten to add, it only becomes *biblical* when we welcome people into our lives who are *different from us*—and thus stretch to enfold them into our lives. Pizza and football with the guys sure is fun, but it's not biblical hospitality.

The Christians in Rome were on the verge of splintering into factions because of disagreements over cultural issues. So Paul challenges them to practice hospitality — *to extend a Christlike welcome to others*: "Therefore welcome one another as Christ has welcomed you, for the glory of God" (Romans 15:7). Wholeness, in this sense, means being Christlike by inviting different kinds of people into your life. As Christ has welcomed you, you now welcome others, for the glory of God.

FAIR-WEATHER CHRISTIANS?

Wholeness also means bearing the full image of Christ in *different situations* in life. Real Christians don't change with the changing of the seasons or with the circumstances of their lives.

Churches can attract fair-weather fans, much like sports teams on a winning streak. There are people who profess Christ but treat him like their "favorite" sports team — they come out for the big games, like Christmas or Easter, or a niece's dedication or a sister's baptism. When God appears to be winning in their life, they're fully supportive and shout louder than anyone. But if God should stop delivering them personal victories, they hop off the bandwagon to join a more promising team.

No one likes fair-weather fans. They're opportunistic; they lack loyalty. To the real fans, those who are faithful through thick and thin, in good seasons and bad, these fair-weather fans aren't fans at all—they're groupies, at best. Sure, they wear the baseball cap, but only because that team made it to the World Series. Next year, who knows.

Jesus exposes these fair-weather Christians in the parable of the sower (see Matthew 13:1–23), when he describes the second and third seeds. Both seeds, he tells us, looked real, but neither one was. This became evident when the circumstances of their lives changed. For some, persecution came and suffocated any enthusiasm there may have been for the kingdom. For others, the cares of this world and deceitfulness of riches strangled their spiritual life, and their commitment to Christ slowly evaporated.

Such is the case with fair-weather Christians. The beautiful thing about Christ is that he doesn't change with circumstances. "Jesus Christ is the same yesterday and today and forever" (Hebrews 13:8). He's no fair-weather fan. Neither are real Christians, who have Christ living in them. They don't jump on the God bandwagon when it's cool or convenient. They don't don the Jesus jersey only when they're celebrating a big win in life.

Real Christians, like the saints John sees in his revelation, follow the Lamb wherever he goes (Revelation 14:4). They're faithful to Jesus in every circumstance and situation. Real Christians are resilient, like the tree depicted in Psalm 1, that yields its fruit in season, and whose leaf does not wither, but prospers all year round (1:3–4). Or to quote the apostle Paul, real Christians, who see all of life in light of the resurrection of Christ, are "steadfast, immovable, always abounding in the work of the Lord, knowing that in the Lord [their] labor is not in vain" (1 Corinthians 15:58).

Christlikeness means you can say with Paul, "I have learned in whatever situation I am to be content. I know how to be brought low, and I know how to abound. In any and every circumstance, I have learned the secret of facing plenty and hunger, abundance and need" (Philippians 4:11–12). In Christ you have found the secret to contentment, and can confess, "I can do all things through him who strengthens me" (verse 13). Even if your work comes unraveled, or a relationship falls apart, or clouds of discouragement won't scatter, you will still rejoice in the Lord, and take joy in the God of your salvation (see Habakkuk 3:17–19).

MY PUNY LITTLE BRANCH

Real Christians are whole people who bear Christ's full image. Their lives are morally and spiritually symmetrical. They aren't lopsided—strong in one area, lacking in others. They won't look distorted, like the figures we see in funhouse mirrors. Instead, they reflect, in varying degrees and ways, the full image of Christ.

But we need to remember that real Christians are also real people. Each has a unique personality and background, unique experiences and influences that make them the person they are. And these factors influence the particular shape of Christlikeness in each Christian. In other words, while real Christians are well-rounded, they aren't perfectly so. Even though you're real, you're still a work in progress. Christlikeness means progress, not perfection.

Remember that growing in Christlikeness doesn't mean striving to make it happen, because it's not ultimately about you but about *Christ in you.* The key to Christlikeness is learning to say with Paul, "I have been crucified with Christ. It is no longer I who live, but Christ who lives in me" (Galatians 2:20).

Hudson Taylor had a good handle on this truth. He called it *living the exchanged life.* He understood that his life as a Christian was all about Christ living within him rather than about him trying to make Christlikeness happen on his own. Writing to his sister, Taylor explains how he wrestled with this discovery:

> All the time I felt assured that there was in Christ all I needed, but the practical question was—how to get it *out.* He was rich truly, but I was poor; he was strong, but I weak. I knew full well that there was in the root, the stem, abundant fatness, but how to get it into my puny little branch was the question.[39]

He continued to grapple with this idea of an exchanged life until eventually light dawned and the Lord gave him insight into what he called his "spiritual secret." He realized it's not about trying harder to live a good Christian life. It's about embracing *by faith* the exchanged life—Christ's life for you, in you. Listen to him explain:

> As I thought of the Vine and the branches, what light the blessed Spirit poured direct into my soul! How great seemed my mistake in wishing to get the sap, the fullness out of him! I saw not only that Jesus will never leave me, but that I am a member of his body, of his flesh and of his bones. The vine is not the root merely, but all—root, stem, branches, twigs, leaves, flower, fruit. And Jesus is not that alone—he is soil and sunshine, air and showers, and ten thousand times more than we have ever dreamed, wished for or needed. Oh, the joy of seeing this truth![40]

Jesus Christ died for our sins and was raised for our salvation. He has given his life for us. We can embrace *by faith* this good news—his life in exchange for ours. And with him living in us, we will find that our lives take on a beautiful wholeness as we bear Christ's image and reflect his likeness.

CHAPTER RESOURCES

QUESTIONS FOR REFLECTION

1. Have you known anyone who displays the full image of Christ in his or her life? Describe this person.

2. What does it mean to be a "single-issue Christian"? Do you find yourself prone to this? In what ways do you tend to get off balance?

3. When you consider the life of Jesus, how would you describe the kind of relationships he had with people? What kinds of people did he spend time with? Where in your life do you see a lack of Christlikeness in relationships?

4. Consider the following statement from the apostle Paul: "I have learned in whatever situation I am to be content. I know how to be brought low, and I know how to abound. In any and every circumstance, I have learned the secret of facing plenty and hunger, abundance and need" (Philippians 4:11 – 12). What role does contentment play in being spiritually whole or Christlike?

5. If maturity is reflecting the life of Christ more consistently in your relationships, your life circumstances, and the things you concern yourself with, then in which area do you feel you need the most growth? How might others help you?

6. Read Galatians 2:20. If becoming more spiritually whole is not about striving to make it happen but about allowing Christ to live in and through you, then how would you encourage someone who feels caught in a circle of always striving?

SCRIPTURES TO PONDER

- Psalm 119
- Matthew 5 – 6
- Ephesians 4 – 6
- Colossians 3 – 4

BOOKS TO HELP YOU DIG DEEPER

Bridges, Jerry. *The Practice of Godliness.* 1983. Reprint, Colorado Springs: NavPress, 2008.

DeYoung, Kevin. *The Hole in Our Holiness: Filling the Gap between Gospel Passion and the Pursuit of Godliness.* Wheaton, IL: Crossway, 2012.

Edwards, Jonathan. *Charity and Its Fruits: Living in the Light of God's Love.* 1852. Edited by Kyle Strobel. Reprint, Wheaton, IL: Crossway, 2012.

Peterson, Eugene H. *A Long Obedience in the Same Direction: Discipleship in an Instant Society.* 1980. Reprint, Colorado Springs: NavPress, 2000.

Ryle, J. C. *Holiness: Its Nature, Hindrances, Difficulties, and Roots.* 1883. Reprint, Peabody, MA: Hendrickson, 2007.

Biographies for Encouragement

Bonar, A. A. *Robert Murray McCheyne: A Biography.* 1960. Reprint, Grand Rapids: Zondervan, 1983.

Metaxas, Eric. *Amazing Grace: William Wilberforce and the Heroic Campaign to End Slavery.* New York: HarperCollins, 2007.

Taylor, Howard and Geraldine. *Hudson Taylor's Spiritual Secret.* 1932. Edited by Gregg Lewis. Reprint, Grand Rapids: Discovery House, 1990.

7
HUNGER: A TORRENT OF SPIRITUAL DESIRE

As a sophomore at Wheaton College, Jim Elliot concluded that God had called him to preach the gospel in Latin America. He wrote his parents in November 1947 to inform them of his decision. This would be a momentous occasion for Jim, more than either he or his parents could have imagined at the time. Ultimately, this decision would cost him his life.

As Jim's letter reveals, he felt compelled to go to Latin America because of a hunger within his soul. "The Lord has given me," he wrote to his parents, "a hunger for righteousness and piety that can alone be of Himself."[41] Jim's desire for more of God caused him to risk all in the jungles of Ecuador. As with so many others who've honored Christ in their generation, Jim Elliot exemplifies the fifth mark of a real Christian — *hunger*.

Hunger shapes the lives of real Christians. It's the secret to their spiritual vibrancy. We see this when we take a closer look at the lives of the psalmists, those who wrote the song-book of the Scriptures. In the lyrics and poems of the Bible we find grittiness and gladness, tears and triumph, sadness and celebration. But more than anything else, we see a hunger for God. Listen to the sounds of their craving:

O God, you are my God; earnestly I seek you;
    my soul thirsts for you;
my flesh faints for you,
    as in a dry and weary land where there is no water.

Psalm 63:1

As a deer pants for flowing streams,
    so pants my soul for you, O God.
My soul thirsts for God,
    for the living God.
When shall I come and appear before God?

Psalm 42:1–2

How lovely is your dwelling place,
    O LORD of hosts!
My soul longs, yes, faints
    for the courts of the LORD;
my heart and flesh sing for joy
    to the living God.

Psalm 84:1–2

After reading the Psalms, A. W. Tozer once wrote, "David's life was *a torrent of spiritual desire*, and his psalms ring with the cry of the seeker and the glad shout of the finder."[42] I must confess that my life, by comparison, often feels more like a trickle than a torrent. Perhaps you can relate. Not every

moment is filled with insatiable longing for God. And yet
Scripture is clear on this—*hunger* is a mark of a real Christian.

REAL HUNGER VERSUS NOT REAL HUNGER

There is a difference between real hunger and what I'll call
"fake" hunger. A real Christian's hunger may begin slowly,
but it will *grow* over time, so that by the end of life a real
Christian is *hungrier* than ever for God.

By contrast, someone who is not real may have hunger
that starts off strong, but it will *diminish* over time, so that
eventually this person is *less* hungry for God, if at all. "Been
there, done that," will be their mentality. Spiritual realities,
whether God or Scripture or worship, will no longer appeal
to them, at least not like they used to. They will no longer
seek after God but will simply coast along, driven not by
desire but by habit or tradition, nostalgia or sentimentality.

Or think about it this way. Those who aren't real only
hunger for God *until* they find him—or at least find what
they are looking for. Once they get from God what they
are looking for, they stop seeking him. On the other hand,
real Christians are truly hungry for one thing—God. They
continue to desire God even *after* they have found him. They
begin to truly seek God only after they've tasted and seen
that the Lord is good (see 1 Peter 2:3).

There is a man in my congregation who is twice my age
but has at least four times my hunger for God. His zeal is
palpable, and his desire for Christ contagious, even though
he's walked with Christ for more than three-quarters of
a century. If the lines on his face and the gray in his hair

weren't revealing, you'd think he was a new convert in his early twenties. I always marvel at his hunger for God, and pray I will also enjoy that same hunger into the winter season of life—and never retire from spiritual desire.

SWEETER THAN HONEY

One of the fascinating things about spiritual hunger is that it can't be hidden. If it's real in your soul, it will reveal itself in your life. You'll see its effects, and so will others. My wife and I know when our four-year-old is hungry—he acts crazy for no apparent reason. Or when our teenage son is rooting around in the kitchen cabinets, we know it's time for dinner. Our kids can't hide their hunger; they don't even try.

But how does hunger for God reveal itself in our lives? Often the first place is with a desire for *the Word of God.* Those who desire God want to hear from God. That's why when the Bible speaks of longing, it's most often longing for God's Word.[43] In Psalm 19, for example, David not only celebrates God's Word but also acknowledges his hunger for it:

> The law of the Lord is perfect,
>   reviving the soul;
> the testimony of the Lord is sure,
>   making wise the simple;
> the precepts of the Lord are right,
>   rejoicing the heart;
> the commandment of the Lord is pure,
>   enlightening the eyes;
> the fear of the Lord is clean,
>   enduring forever;

the rules of the LORD are true,
    and righteous altogether.
More to be desired are they than gold,
    even much fine gold;
sweeter also than honey
    and drippings of the honeycomb.

Psalm 19:7–10

If your hunger is real, you'll desire, like David, more and more of the Word of God. You won't be satisfied with what you already know of the Bible, what you learned in Sunday school, what you picked up at Bible college. No, you'll be greedy for more Bible, eager to consume Scripture, ready to taste the treasures of God's Word.

Of course, you should not expect to hunger for God's Word if you don't read it. Nor can you expect to grow in your desire for Scripture if you read only with your eyes and not with your heart. Words can travel from the page of Scripture to our minds, but if they don't settle in our souls, we won't grow in our desire for God.

Whenever we open God's Word, we ought to pray for the Holy Spirit to give us light so we can see the spiritual realities to which Scripture points. "Open my eyes," the psalmist wisely pleads, "that I may behold wondrous things out of your law" (Psalm 119:18).

"FOOD THAT YOU DON'T KNOW ABOUT"

Real Christians also hunger to do *the will of God*. They find obedience satisfying. Like Jim Elliot, this is what animates their lives, motivates their decisions, enlivens their desires, and guides their choices.

As Jesus passed through Samaria, he found rest beside a well and spoke to a woman about her soul. His disciples, upon returning, found their Lord chatting with the woman and marveled because of it. They also urged him to take some food. "Rabbi, eat," they said. But Jesus replied, "I have food to eat that you do not know about" (John 4:31–32).

Naturally, this intensified the disciples' curiosity, leaving them to wonder whether he called for carryout or had a pizza delivered. Jesus knew they were baffled, and he dispelled their confusion by clarifying the nature of his hunger—and the source of its satisfaction. "My food," he told them, "is to do the will of him who sent me and to accomplish his work" (John 4:34).

Real hunger, the kind we see in Jesus, is hunger to do God's will, which means a hunger for *holiness*. For when you boil it all down, holiness *is* God's will for us. "For this is the will of God, your sanctification," Paul writes, "that you abstain from sexual immorality; that each one of you know how to control his own body in holiness and honor, not in the passion of lust like the Gentiles who do not know God … For God has not called us for impurity, but *in holiness*" (1 Thessalonians 4:3–5, 7, emphasis added).

This also means there will be an intense dislike of sin—we might call it *hatred* of sin. Those who have tasted and seen that the Lord is good want to rid their lives of anything that hinders their ability to feed on God. In fact, they go to war against the sin in their life, so they can more easily satisfy their hunger for God. "A godly man is a mortal enemy to his sin," explains Jonathan Edwards. "Nothing will satisfy him, but his life is, as it were, bloodthirsty towards sin."[44]

We ought to ask ourselves, then, whether our hunger for God and for holiness is real enough to cause us to hate the sin in our life. Are we bloodthirsty for the death of sin? Or are we content simply to shoot spitballs at it, hoping eventually that sin will just leave us alone?

LABORING FOR WHAT WON'T PERISH

Genuine longing for God expresses itself in living for God — accomplishing the work God has given you to do. If your hunger is real, you will desire *the work of God*.

After feeding a large crowd, Jesus told them they only pursued him because their bellies were satisfied — "You ate your fill of the loaves," he said (John 6:26). But Jesus also cautioned the crowds, "Do not work for the food that perishes, but for the food that endures to eternal life, which the Son of Man will give to you" (verse 27). They then asked him the all-important question: "What must we do, to be doing the works of God?" (verse 28). "This is the work of God," Jesus replied, "that you believe in him whom he has sent" (verse 29).

To know Christ and make him known — this is the work God has for us. Real hunger for God is thus a hunger *to witness*. If you truly desire God, you will want more and more people to join you in your hunger for him. You won't be satisfied keeping God to yourself. In fact, you will want others to join you, so that your own joy in God will be both multiplied and intensified. A shared joy is a doubled joy!*

---

* I owe this way of putting things to Daniel Fuller and John Piper.

Remember, genuine hunger for God is the best starting point for evangelism. If you struggle to share your faith with others, the simplest place to start is by sharing with others the impact that hunger for God has on your life. People may not listen to arguments, but they will take note of an insatiable craving for something grand. Christians who are content with the world's half-baked goods will get little notice. But a soul that yearns for Jesus is a compelling witness in a starving world.

PANTING FOR FLOWING STREAMS

But perhaps more than anything else, hunger for God reveals itself in hunger for *the worship of God*. A soul that longs for more of God sounds like this: "As a deer pants for flowing streams, so pants my soul for you, O God. My soul thirsts for God, for the living God" (Psalm 42:1–2). But when you're burdened with this sort of desire, you also ask with the psalmist, "When shall I come and appear before God?" (verse 2).

The heart that hungers for God knows there's only one way to satisfy that hunger—with worship. "How lovely is your dwelling place, O LORD of hosts! My soul longs, yes, faints for the courts of the LORD; my heart and flesh sing for joy to the living God" (Psalm 84:1–2). Hunger for God will cause you to confess, "For a day in your courts is better than a thousand elsewhere. I would rather be a doorkeeper in the house of my God than dwell in the tents of wickedness" (verse 10).

If you hunger for God, you'll approach the gathering of believers on the Lord's Day, not as a well-worn routine, but as a great feast. Church won't be optional, but essential. You'll come to the table of worship each week eager to have your hunger not only satisfied but intensified. You'll realize that by sharing your hunger with others, you'll multiply it, deepen it, strengthen it. And not only will you go away having fed on Christ; you'll leave hungering for more of him.

If you hunger for the worship of God, you will also hunger for heaven. For that is what heaven is—a *world of worship* where we will be free from the deadening burden of sin and able to breathe the crisp, clean air of holiness. Hunger will make you envious of the scenes you find in the book of Revelation, where innumerable saints and myriads of angels are gathered around God's throne, worshiping the Lamb.

> Then I looked, and I heard around the throne and the living creatures and the elders the voice of many angels, numbering myriads of myriads and thousands of thousands, saying with a loud voice, "Worthy is the Lamb who was slain, to receive power and wealth and wisdom and might and honor and glory and blessing!" And I heard every creature in heaven and on earth and under the earth and in the sea, and all that is in them, saying, "To him who sits on the throne and to the Lamb be blessing and honor and glory and might forever and ever!" And the four living creatures said, "Amen!" and the elders fell down and worshiped.
>
> Revelation 5:11–14

A real Christian is one in whom hunger for God grows, beginning with the small flicker that arrives with new birth and increasing into a campfire of affection that generates enough heat to warm you and others. But as you continue to stoke this fire of affection, it becomes a veritable bonfire. Eventually, you will see the Grand Object of your desire, the face of Jesus in all of his resplendent beauty and grace, and your life will be set ablaze with God-centered longing and delight—forever and ever! This is the glorious future of the Christian's hunger for God.

DEVELOPING YOUR HUNGER FOR GOD

But what if you don't have any real hunger for God? The first step is to be honest with yourself. It's good to acknowledge that you don't desire God as you ought. There's no sense in pretending. Nor is there any need to try to convince yourself you're in a better place than you really are. Why not ask God for mercy rather than pretend you're fine?

None of us, of course, hunger for God as we ought. This is one of the devastating effects of the fall—sin destroys our appetite for God. To be sure, fallen humanity still hungers for the *things* of God—what God can do for us or give to us, whether health, wealth, peace, security, well-being, rest, or even eternal life. This is why some folks are indeed eager to come to church; they're seeking the things of God, a sense of well-being, a fix to a broken relationship, or healing for a personal loss.

But the question we must ask is, "Am I hungry for God?" Because a hunger for *God's gifts* isn't to be equated with a hunger for *God himself.* To desire what God can do for you is different than to desire who God is in himself—the beauty of his holiness, the glory of his character.

This is why real hunger for God only comes with new birth. Only then is a person given a taste for the goodness of God, the sweetness of his character, the beauty of his holiness.

For some who are reading this book, you may need to be born again before you will have any real hunger for God. And so you need to turn to Christ in repentance and faith, and ask him to give you new birth and a new hunger for God.[45]

HUNGER SATISFIED AND INTENSIFIED

But let's assume, at this point, that your hunger for God is real. How do you increase it? First, you need to understand this paradoxical truth about hunger for God: *When it is fed, spiritual hunger doesn't go away; it grows.* When you have what you want, your hunger isn't simply satisfied; it's intensified. Unlike physical hunger, which when fed is satisfied, when you feed on God, your hunger for God increases.

For those of you who do have real hunger for God, let me encourage you to go ahead and *glut yourself* on God. Yes, that's right. Don't hold back. Indulge yourself as much as possible. Throw off constraints. Give yourself entirely to satisfying your hunger for God—with God himself.

In fact, don't worry about rationing God—only enjoying a little now so you'll have some for later. God is an infinite ocean of delights and can never run dry or be used up. "You make known to me the path of life," is the psalmist's glad confession. "In your presence there is fullness of joy; at your right hand are pleasures forevermore" (Psalm 16:11).

And don't fret about overindulging in too much of God, as though you could get sick of God. Hunger for God doesn't work like that. In fact, what you'll find is the more you feed on him, the sweeter he becomes. Make it your ambition, then, to feed on God as much as possible. You will not be disappointed.

REAL CHRISTIANS ARE SEEKERS

Regrettably, we're in danger these days of downplaying the importance of hunger for God. It happens innocently enough. Within an evangelical subculture, we have unwittingly transferred the language of "seeking" God from the Christian to the *non-Christian*. If we gauge things by how we speak, we would conclude that it's the non-Christians who seek God, while real Christians don't.

Nearly fifty years ago, A. W. Tozer spotted the danger in this way of thinking. He warned that Christians had been snared in spurious logic—logic that goes like this: *If you've found God, you no longer need to seek him.*[46] But this thinking is devastating to real Christianity. For as Tozer explains, "Christ may be 'received' without creating any special love for Him in the soul of the receiver. The man is 'saved,' but he is not hungry or thirsty after God. In fact, he is specifically taught to be satisfied and is encouraged to be content with little."[47]

At the end of the day, the only true seekers are real Christians who have tasted and seen that the Lord is good. They know the sweetness of the glory of God and aren't content with what they've had. They want more. Like the apostle

Paul, they're always "forgetting what lies behind and straining forward to what lies ahead" (Philippians 3:13).

Thus their lives are marked by a holy dissatisfaction and a hunger for more of God. They know there is so much more of Christ to see, so much more to experience of God's grace and love. And so this is how the real Christian continually prays:

> O God, the Triune God, I want to want Thee; I long to be filled with longing; I thirst to be made more thirsty still. Show me Thy glory, I pray Thee, that so I may know Thee indeed. Begin in mercy a new work of love within me. Say to my soul, "Rise up, my love, my fair one, and come away." Then give me grace to rise and follow Thee up from this misty lowland where I have wandered so long. In Jesus' name. Amen.[48]

CHAPTER RESOURCES

QUESTIONS FOR REFLECTION

1. Would you describe yourself as someone who is hungry for God? How have you seen yourself grow in your hunger for God? What has contributed most to this growth?

2. Read Psalm 19:7 – 10. Why does the psalmist desire God's Word? How do you read the Bible, not only with your eyes, but also with your heart? How would you encourage someone who is an occasional Bible reader, but wishes they could read it more regularly?

3. Read 1 Thessalonians 4:2 – 7. Would you agree that doing the will of God is what satisfies the soul? Why is a posture of an intense dislike of the sin in your own life critical to doing the will of God?

4. We also hunger for God by doing the work of God — *to know Jesus Christ and to make him known in the world.* Is there work that God is calling you to do? How can you help or encourage others in this?

5. Read Psalm 84:1 – 2 and Revelation 5:11 – 14. Describe the relationship between a hunger for God and the worship of God. Why is it that if you hunger for the worship of God, you will hunger for heaven? Are there ways that you purposely express worship to God on a regular basis? If so, what are they?

SCRIPTURES TO PONDER

- Psalms 19:7 – 10; 63:1 – 11; 42:1 – 2; 82:1 – 2
- Song of Solomon
- John 17
- Philippians 3
- Revelation 4 – 5; 21 – 22

BOOKS TO HELP YOU DIG DEEPER

Piper, John. *Desiring God: Meditations of a Christian Hedonist*. 1996. Reprint, Colorado Springs: Multnomah, 2011.

———. *When I Don't Desire God: How to Fight for Joy*. Wheaton, IL: Crossway, 2004.

Tozer, A. W. *The Pursuit of God*. Harrisburg, PA: Christian Publications, 1948.

Biographies for Encouragement

Augustine, *Confessions*. 397. Translated by Gary Wills. Reprint, New York: Penguin, 2006.

Lewis, C. S. *Surprised by Joy*. 1955. Reprint, New York: HarperCollins, 2010.

Sargent, John, *Life and Letters of Henry Martyn*. 1819. Reprint, Carlisle, PA: Banner of Truth, 1985.

8
PERFECTED LOVE: THE MARK OF MARKS

On June 2, 1939, a young German pastor by the name of Dietrich Bonhoeffer set sail for New York City. This was his second visit to the United States, and he planned to stay for at least a year. But as soon as he arrived in America, he felt a strong prompting to return to Germany. Although things had taken a turn for the worse in Germany, Bonhoeffer wanted to return and identify with his countrymen in their struggle against the Nazis.

Shortly after his arrival, Bonhoeffer wrote a letter to a friend back in Germany, confessing his change of heart and change of plans:

> I have had time to think and to pray about my situation and that of my nation and to have God's will for me clarified. I have come to the conclusion that I have made a mistake in coming to America. I must live through this difficult period of our national history with the Christian people of Germany.[49]

Bonhoeffer was only in the United States for a month

when he boarded a ship and returned to Germany. One historian describes the decision:

> The image of Bonhoeffer boarding ship, voluntarily preparing to sail back—straight into the hell that Germany had become, into resistance, into the great likelihood of his own death—is an unforgettable scene and a poignant moment in the history of the Church in the twentieth century.[50]

The famous British journalist Malcolm Muggeridge described Bonhoeffer's decision with characteristic grace: "Had he stayed, America might have gained a theologian, but the world would have lost a Christian martyr."[51] Not only is this true, but we would have lost one of the twentieth-century's most profound examples of our sixth mark of "real"—*perfected love.*

THE MARK OF MARKS

The authors of the New Testament are clear about what it means to be real. Perhaps no writer stated this difference more starkly than the apostle John, the beloved disciple and author of the fourth gospel, Revelation, and three potent little letters. Here's a sample of what he says in his first letter, where he distinguishes between those who are real and those who aren't:

> This is the message we have heard from him and proclaim to you, that God is light, and in him is no darkness at all. If we say we have fellowship with him while we walk in darkness, we lie and do not practice the truth.
>
> 1 John 1:5–6

Whoever says "I know him" but does not keep his commandments is a liar, and the truth is not in him, but whoever keeps his word, in him truly the love of God is perfected. By this we may know that we are in him.

1 John 2:4–5

Little children, let no one deceive you. Whoever practices righteousness is righteous, as he is righteous. Whoever makes a practice of sinning is of the devil, for the devil has been sinning from the beginning. The reason the Son of God appeared was to destroy the works of the devil.

1 John 3:7–8

John captures the essence of what it means to be a real Christian with a single phrase—*perfected love*: "No one has ever seen God; if we love one another, God abides in us and his love is *perfected* in us" (1 John 4:12, emphasis added). We read a few verses later:

By this is love *perfected* with us, so that we may have confidence for the day of judgment, because as he is so also are we in this world. There is no fear in love, but *perfect* love casts out fear. For fear has to do with punishment, and whoever fears has not been *perfected* in love.

1 John 4:17–18, emphasis added

This perfected love of which John speaks is what I call the mark of marks, because it is the most reliable way to know if you're real, *the surest evidence of authentic faith*. The late Francis

Schaeffer called it simply "the badge Christ gave."[52] In addition, all the other marks of a real Christian, from humility to hunger, *express themselves in love*, or are different ways in which love works itself out in our lives. Furthermore, perfected love is *the goal of the other marks*. Each of the other marks of authentic Christian faith is given to us and designed to promote perfected love. Humility subverts pride and frees us to love others, irrespective of who they are. Meekness empowers us to love people, regardless of how they've treated us. Contrition inspires love for holiness over love for sin. Wholeness, or Christlikeness, helps us see blind spots so we can better love others. And hunger for God motivates us to seek after the One who has loved us and given himself for us — and who now challenges us to go and do the same for others.

VISIBLE, TANGIBLE, PRACTICAL, SACRIFICIAL

But what is perfected love? It is, first of all, *visible* love — love that's gone public. It's love, not as an unseen feeling, but as a known fact. It's *tangible*. Not only can it be seen; it can be touched. This is because perfected love is *practical*, the kind of love that meets real, concrete needs. And because it's tangible and practical, perfected love is *sacrificial*. It's costly, as we give of ourselves for the sake of others.

One of the most heartening truths of Scripture is this: "God is love" (1 John 4:8). But did you know that God's love is what John calls perfected love? God is a community of persons — Father, Son, and Holy Spirit. Because of this, God is never alone, but always enjoys relationship within himself, between the three persons of the Godhead. And this Trinitarian relationship is marked, above all things, by love.

Remarkably, this perfect Trinitarian love has gone public in the person of the Son, who is the expression of God's perfected love. For God's love was made visible, tangible, practical, and sacrificial in and through the incarnation. "In this the love of God was made manifest among us," John tells us, "that God sent his only Son into the world" (1 John 4:9).

Taking a cue from the apostle John, we might even say that God *perfected* his love by sending his Son into the world. Not that God's love was ever less than perfect! What I mean is that by sending his Son, God went public with his love. The Father's love became perfected — made known to all — in the person of Jesus. This is the profound point John makes in the opening of his letter:

> That which was from the beginning, which we have heard, which we have seen with our eyes, which we looked upon and have touched with our hands, concerning the word of life — the life was made manifest, and we have seen it, and testify to it and proclaim to you the eternal life, which was with the Father and was made manifest to us — that which we have seen and heard we proclaim also to you, so that you too may have fellowship with us; and indeed our fellowship is with the Father and with his Son Jesus Christ.
>
> 1 John 1:1–3

Perfected love is the person of Christ. In Jesus we see God's love for the world: "By this we know love, that he laid down his life for us" (1 John 3:16). Jesus is the love of God made visible, tangible, practical, and sacrificial. The incarnate Son of God is the Father's love perfected in and for the world.

PERFECTED LOVE IS FROM ABOVE

We understand, then, that God's love is perfected love. But we also ought to realize that perfected love *comes from* God. John is clear on this point: "for love is from God" (1 John 4:7). The love of real Christians isn't something they muster up on their own. Anyone who knows real love will tell you that you can't just make it up.

Perfected love comes not from below, but from above. Its source is in God alone. God is the one who initiates love, and he is the giver of love: "In this is love, not that we have loved God but that he loved us and sent his Son to be the propitiation for our sins" (1 John 4:10). And John adds, "We love because he first loved us" (verse 19).

God is also the one who *defines* love — not through the use of a dictionary, but by means of setting forth a living pattern in Jesus. God empowers perfected love through the gift of the Spirit. Perfected love is a fruit of the Spirit (see Galatians 5:22–23). Indeed, the Spirit is the love the Father has for the Son, and the Son for the Father. And so, as John writes, "We know that we abide in him and he in us, because he has given us of his Spirit" (1 John 4:13). As we embrace the Father's love in the person of Christ, we come to know God and are filled, the Bible says, with his own perfected love through the Holy Spirit (see Romans 5:5). Miracle of miracles!

LOVING GOD FOR NO OTHER REASON

The Bible teaches that real love flows from faith — from seeing the glory of God in the face of Jesus Christ (see 2 Corinthians 4:6). When the veil is lifted and we see God's glory as that which is beautiful in itself, our heart is enlivened with love for God. We see him as lovely, and therefore love him. This is the foundation of genuine love for God — *to love God for no other reason than because God is lovely.*

To be sure, real Christians love God because God loves them. But they also, and more importantly, love God because of who God is in himself. Non-Christians, however, "love" God *only* because God loves them. Since they've not received new birth, and thus can't see the beauty of God in the face of Jesus Christ, they don't love God for God's own sake, or simply because of who he is. Instead, they "love" God only because of what God has done for them.

But to love God only or ultimately because he loves you is really no different than what pagans do. Do you remember what Jesus says about loving your enemies? "If you love those who love you, what benefit is that to you? For even sinners," he went on to say, "love those who love them" (Luke 6:32). If you love God simply because he loves you, it is no benefit to you — *even those who don't know Christ do that*, Jesus says.

This was, you may recall, what Satan suspected of Job. Satan was convinced that Job's great piety and love for God was not all that great, but rather self-serving at the core. In other words, he suspected that Job loved God because God took good care of Job. Thus the Lord says to Satan, "Have you considered my servant Job, that there is none like him on the earth, a blameless and upright man, who fears God and turns away from evil?" (Job 1:8). Satan, of course, has doubts, and so he says incredulously to God, "Does Job fear God for no reason?" (verse 9).

You may know how this story unfolds. The Lord, in his severe mercy toward Job, allows Satan to harm him mercilessly, seeking to destroy his life, but more importantly, to devour his faith. Satan thinks that if every good thing in Job's life is stripped away, then Job will stop loving God. Satan assumes that Job loves God for a reason — namely, because God loves Job.

But by the end of the book, what we find is this: Job's confession of love for God is rooted in the beauty of who God is rather than in what God has done for Job. Thus, the affirmation of the opening chapter shows itself true in Job's own life: "Naked I came from my mother's womb, and naked shall I return. The LORD gave, and the LORD has taken away; blessed be the name of the LORD" (Job 1:21).

When you say that, you make it crystal clear that you love God for no other reason than that God is lovely and thus worthy of love. And that is why true love for God in the heart of a real Christian is such a powerful and persevering thing. When tribulations come for the sake of the name, or when the cares of this world crop up all around, those with counterfeit or feigned love fall away. But those with real love will persevere because their love is rooted in who God is.

Please don't misunderstand this point! It's certainly not wrong to love God because God loves you. In fact, it's absolutely essential. In light of all that God has done for us in Jesus Christ, what else could we do but love him? As the apostle John reminds us, "We love because he first loved us" (1 John 4:19). Or as the psalmist writes, "I love the LORD, because he has heard my voice and my pleas for mercy" (Psalm 116:1).

Yet the telltale sign of whether your love for God is ultimately rooted in his loveliness is whether you endure difficulty well. When you are able to endure suffering like Job, without cursing God, you know you have come to love God. You love him, not because he's your sugar daddy, but because he has become beautiful to you. If God can wound you deeply yet still have your heart, then you have come to love him for his sake, not simply for your own.

THE CHALLENGE OF IMPERFECTED LOVE

At this point, we should also mention the challenge of *imperfected love*. This is love in thought, but not in practice. Imperfected love isn't bad; it's just incomplete. It's good in principle; it just hasn't reached its goal.

Apple seeds, of course, aren't bad. It's just that if you're trying to get apples, seeds alone don't get you there; they're incomplete. They're imperfected, so to speak, because they've not yet reached their goal — bearing fruit. The seed contains the fruit in principle but not yet in fact.

The same is true for real Christians. John challenges us to move beyond imperfected love to perfected love: "Little children, let us not love in word or talk but in deed and in truth" (1 John 3:18). Imperfected love is love in word or talk only. It's love that doesn't go beyond good intentions to sacrificial service. It's wanting to love, but not actually loving. Imperfected love is when you say, "I love God," and yet don't meet the concrete needs of your brother or sister (see 1 John 4:20).

Growing in Christ means continuing to see our imperfected love grow to perfected love — that is, to see love exert more control over our lives. "By this my Father is glorified, that you bear much fruit and so prove to be my disciples" (John 15:8). Bearing fruit is all about moving from imperfected to perfected love. It's not about mustering up love in our lives. Rather, it's about letting the love that God has shed abroad in our hearts go public for the good of others.

THE GREATEST OF THESE IS LOVE

But how do you do this? How do you turn imperfected love into perfected love? First, we can *prioritize* perfected love. There are many excellent things we should pursue in the Christian life — deeper spiritual experience, risky acts of faith, greater understanding of biblical truth. But above all, unchallenged in importance, is the call to perfected love. In Paul's words, "So now faith, hope, and love abide, these three; but the greatest of these is love" (1 Corinthians 13:13). Or as one of the great preachers of the twentieth century said, "The hallmark of the saints is their great, increasing concern about the element of love in their lives."[53]

Oswald Chambers, in his classic *My Utmost for His Highest*, has a delightful way of describing what it means to prioritize love. In his words, we should so prioritize our relationship with Christ, and abide in his love, that we become "carefully careless about everything else in comparison to that."[54]

Often what hinders love from reaching its goal in our lives

is insecurity; we know perfected love can push us into awkward spots and messy situations. We give more than we can afford, involve ourselves in the lives of others in ways that take us out of our comfort zones, or take on a responsibility at significant cost to ourselves or our family—the sacrifices of perfected love. When we pursue perfected love, we're inevitably led into places where we feel vulnerable and exposed, situations where we're forced to cast ourselves on the grace of God for help—which ultimately is a great place to be.

"ABIDE IN ME"

We can also *protect* perfected love. And we need to, because it's possible to lose our first love. This is what happened to the otherwise admirable church in Ephesus. They were exemplary in so many respects—faithful, discerning, strong in the face of opposition. "But," Jesus says to them, "I have this against you, that you have abandoned the love you had at first" (Revelation 2:4).

Love for Christ can slip; it can grow cold. This usually happens without us even knowing it, like the temperature outside falling below zero while we sleep in our comfy bed. So we must protect perfected love, which we do by guarding our heart and being careful about what we love. In John's first epistle, he cautions, "Do not love the world or the things in the world" (1 John 2:15). He knows that if we share our love with the things of the world, we may eventually lose our love.

Jesus spoke repeatedly of the necessity of *abiding* in him as the key to persevering in perfected love. Because we're nothing more than branches, we can't do much on our own. "Abide in me, and I in you," Jesus says. "As the branch cannot bear fruit by itself, unless it abides in the vine, neither can you, unless you abide in me" (John 15:4). Abiding in Jesus is a prerequisite to perfected love.

CONSIDER HOW TO STIR UP

We will also need the help of others if we're going to promote perfected love in our lives. The author of Hebrews thus encourages us: "And let us consider how to stir up one another to love and good works" (10:24). This verse calls us to think carefully about how we can promote perfected love in each other's lives. Literally, it reads, "And let us consider *one another*, to stir up to love and good works." It's a call to get to know one another so we can better understand how to promote perfected love in our lives.

God has been gracious to me by surrounding me with those who know and love me, and who seek to promote perfected love in my life. First of all, my wife knows me, and she knows how to prod and affirm in a way that catalyzes perfected love in my life. And I think of ministry colleagues who often do the same. I also have close friends who inspire and encourage me in the way of love.

Cultivating perfected love is a community effort, not a one-man show. It takes a whole network of people, a church community, a family of followers of Jesus, to stand by you, to cheer for you, and, when necessary, to challenge you toward greater love for God and others.

MORE LOVE TO THEE!

Finally, if we want to see perfected love flourish in our lives, we ought to *pray* for it. It's tempting to assume we shoulder the responsibility for perfected love. While living a life of love is something we do, we must realize that perfected love is also *God's gift*—something he gives in increasing measure as we ask him for it.

The apostle Paul routinely prays for believers to grow in their love for Christ and one another. "And it is my prayer," he writes to the Philippians, "that your love may abound more and more" (Philippians 1:9). Or for the believers in Thessalonica Paul prays, "May the Lord make you increase and abound in love for one another and for all" (1 Thessalonians 3:12).

When I was a freshman at Wheaton College, God visited the campus in a powerful way. Some even referred to it as a revival.[55] Students gathered for a week straight, eight to ten hours at a time, to worship God and confess sin. During one of the sessions, the college chaplain challenged us to meditate on and memorize Paul's glorious prayer for perfected love from Ephesians 3, that we might indeed grow in love.

For this reason I bow my knees before the Father, from whom every family in heaven and on earth is named, that according to the riches of his glory he may grant you to be strengthened with power through his Spirit in your inner being, so that Christ may dwell in your hearts through faith—that you, being rooted and grounded in love, may have strength to comprehend with all the saints what is the breadth and length and height and depth, and to know the love of Christ that surpasses knowledge, that you may be filled with all the fullness of God.

Ephesians 3:14–19

D. Martyn Lloyd-Jones, former pastor of Westminster Chapel in London, made this observation: "The servants of God who have most adorned the life and the history of the Christian Church have always been men [and women] who have realized that this [knowledge of the love of Christ] is the most important thing of all, and they have spent hours in prayer seeking His face and enjoying His love."[56] Amen to that.

Years ago, a godly woman named Elizabeth Prentiss was suffering from a serious illness. During her convalescence, she wrote a prayer to Christ for more and more love for him. She kept the prayer to herself for many years. Eventually, more than a decade later, she showed the prayer to her husband, who was so moved by what she penned that he encouraged her to publish it. And, thankfully, she did, because her prayer became the text to the wonderful hymn, "More Love to Thee, O Christ."

More love to Thee, O Christ, more love to Thee!
Hear Thou the prayer I make on bended knee.
This is my earnest plea: More love, O Christ, to Thee;
More love to Thee, more love to Thee!

If we're serious about seeing perfected love blossom in our own lives, we ought to pray like Elizabeth Prentiss — *More love to Thee, O Christ, more love to Thee!*

PERFECTED LOVE AND FINAL JUDGMENT

As we grow in perfected love, we not only bless those around us, but also boost our own confidence in the outcome of the last day. In fact, the apostle John says that when we see perfected love in our lives, we can look to the final judgment with optimism rather than anxiety:[*]

> By this is love perfected with us, so that we may have confidence for the day of judgment, because as he is so also are we in this world. There is no fear in love, but perfect love casts out fear. For fear has to do with punishment, and whoever fears has not been perfected in love.
>
> 1 John 4:17 – 18

On the other hand, if you lack perfected love, you ought to fear the final judgment. Even though you may profess faith, if your life doesn't bear the marks of faith, you won't pass muster on the last day. For Scripture insists that judgment is according to works — not according to words, but deeds; not according to intentions, but actions: "For we must all appear before the judgment seat of Christ, so that each one may receive what is due for what he has done in the body, whether good or evil" (2 Corinthians 5:10).[†]

Perfected love is, then, the mark of marks not only for us, but for God. In fact, when God opens the books and sits in judgment, he will look for perfected love in our lives — visible, tangible, practical, sacrificial acts of service done in Jesus' name for the good of others. Or as Jesus says, when

---

[*] For a similar line of thought, see 1 John 2:28 – 29; 3:18 – 22.
[†] See also especially Romans 14:8 – 10.

the Son of Man comes, he will separate the sheep from the goats according to the presence or the absence of perfected love in their lives (see Matthew 25:31–46). A cup of cold water given in Jesus' name will be the mark of marks Christ is looking for on the last day.

WE OUGHT ALSO TO LOVE ONE ANOTHER

One of my dear friends, a pastor in North Carolina, knows a family that recently returned from China with a newly adopted little girl. When they went to the orphanage, what broke their hearts was what they saw—rooms full of orphaned boys and girls wearing bibs that read, "Mommy loves me," or "Daddy loves me."

Each one of these children is waiting for perfected love—love not in word or talk, but in deed and in truth—a love that has become visible, tangible, practical, and sacrificial; a love that has gone public for the good of others.

This is the kind of love our world desperately needs. It's the kind of love the Father has shown us in sending his Son to die for our sins. And it's the kind of love that ought to mark our lives as followers of Jesus. As the apostle John simply yet elegantly puts it, "Beloved, if God so loved us, we also ought to love one another" (1 John 4:11).

CHAPTER RESOURCES

QUESTIONS FOR REFLECTION

1. Why is perfected love the clearest and most reliable way to know whether you are a real Christian?

2. Read John 15:4–11. Jesus calls us to abide in him, and says that apart from him we can do nothing — at least nothing of lasting value or eternal impact. In verse 9, he calls us to abide in his love. If someone were to observe the fruit of your abiding in God's love, what would be their reaction? How would the fruit appear?

3. Read Hebrews 10:24–25. Why is it that we need the help of others to promote perfected love in our lives? What are tangible ways you have seen people stirring up one another to love?

4. Read Philippians 1:9. Do you pray for your love and the love of others to abound more and more? If so, are there people or circumstances you specifically pray for? If not, what steps can you take to grow in this way?

5. Read John 13:1. Even though Jesus' hour had come, he loved his disciples to the end. How does Jesus' perfected love manifest itself in this passage? Reflect on how you can demonstrate this Christlike love to others.

SCRIPTURES TO PONDER

- John 13
- Romans 12–15
- 1 Corinthians 12–14
- James
- 1 John

BOOKS TO HELP YOU DIG DEEPER

Chan, Francis. *Crazy Love: Overwhelmed by a Relentless God*. Colorado Springs: Cook, 2008.

Edwards, Jonathan. *Charity and Its Fruits: Living in Light of God's Love*. 1852. Edited by Kyle Strobel. Reprint, Wheaton, IL: Crossway, 2012.

Platt, David. *Radical: Taking Your Faith Back from the American Dream*. Colorado Springs: Multnomah, 2010.

Schaeffer, Francis A. *The Mark of a Christian*. Downers Grove, IL: InterVarsity, 1970.

Strauch, Alexander. *Love or Die: Christ's Wake-Up Call to the Church: Revelation 2:4*. Littleton, CO: Lewis and Roth, 1999.

Biographies for Encouragement

Elliot, Elisabeth. *A Chance to Die: The Life and Legacy of Amy Carmichael*. Old Tappan, NJ: Revell, 1987.

Metaxas, Eric. *Bonhoeffer: Pastor, Martyr, Prophet, Spy*. Nashville: Nelson, 2010.

Pierson, Arthur T. *George Müller of Bristol: His Life of Prayer and Faith*. 1899. Reprint, Grand Rapids: Kregel, 1999.

9
PERSEVERANCE
IS PROOF

Protestant Christianity faces a crisis. Young people are leaving the church in droves. Seven in ten evangelicals stop attending church by age twenty-three, and less than half of them ever return.[57] Think about what that means for a moment. One out of every four kids in your church's youth group is likely to eventually abandon the Christian faith. Or to bring it even closer to home: if you have four children, chances are one will leave the fold and never come back.

The Southern Baptist Convention, America's largest Protestant denomination, claims sixteen million members. This means sixteen million people who have professed faith and been baptized. And yet researchers have found that on any given Sunday, only six of these sixteen million baptized, professing Christians are in church—which leaves ten million missing in worship every week.[58]

So where are they? Are they sleeping in, playing golf, or having brunch? Or have they stopped following Jesus? Are they no longer continuing in the faith? Have they failed to persevere to the end?

You know the old adage — "the proof of the pudding is in the eating." So it is for real Christians. *The proof is in the perseverance.* Or as Charles Spurgeon writes, "Perseverance is the badge of true saints. It is their Scriptural mark."[59]

As we've seen throughout this book, real Christians bear a variety of marks, but *perseverance proves them all.* Perseverance proves humility is real, because humility safeguards our souls from the sin of pride. Perseverance proves meekness is real, because meekness enables us to endure in the face of unjust criticism. Perseverance proves contrition is real, because contrition softens our hearts so we're not hardened by the deceitfulness of sin. Perseverance proves Christlikeness is real, because Christlikeness keeps us from drifting into extremes of one kind or another. And perseverance proves hunger for God is real, because hunger causes us to continually seek after God, and never lose heart.

Jesus says we must persevere to enter the kingdom of God, even though in this hostile world it won't be easy: "You will be hated by all for my name's sake. But the one who endures to the end will be saved" (Mark 13:13). To persecuted believers Jesus likewise promises, "To the one who conquers I will grant to eat of the tree of life, which is in the paradise of God" (Revelation 2:7).

Imagine your pastor has asked you to speak to a group of new Christians at your church. Some were raised in Christian homes; others weren't. But they all appear to be soundly converted and genuinely on fire for Jesus. Your assignment is to encourage them in their newfound faith. What do you say?

The earliest Christians faced this situation countless times, and they usually said the same thing to new converts: *Continue in the faith.*

> When [Barnabas] came [to Antioch] and saw the grace of God, he was glad, and he exhorted them all to *remain faithful* to the Lord with steadfast purpose.
>
> Acts 11:23, emphasis added

> And after the meeting of the synagogue broke up, many Jews and devout converts to Judaism followed Paul and Barnabas, who, as they spoke with them, urged them to *continue in the grace of God.*
>
> Acts 13:43, emphasis added

> When [Paul and Barnabas] had preached the gospel to that city and had made many disciples, they returned to Lystra and to Iconium and to Antioch, strengthening the souls of the disciples, encouraging them to *continue in the faith*, and saying that through many tribulations we must enter the kingdom of God.
>
> Acts 14:21–22, emphasis added

Real Christians persevere in the faith. If you're real, you'll arrive at the end of life and join the apostle Paul in saying: "I have fought the good fight, I have finished the race, I have kept the faith" (2 Timothy 4:7). And on that day those won't be mere words, but cross-purchased, Spirit-wrought, hard-fought-for realities in your life.

FIGHT THE GOOD FIGHT

"A Christian's career is always fighting, never ceasing," observes Charles Spurgeon, "always ploughing the stormy sea, and never resting till he reaches the port of glory."[60] Real Christians, like the apostle Paul, fight the good fight of faith and don't give up. Even though Paul is confident in the Lord, he still wages war against unbelief every single day, "lest after preaching to others I myself should be disqualified" (1 Corinthians 9:27).

Paul is constantly engaged in the fight of faith because he knows the subtlety of sin. He sees how sin works in his own soul; he also sees how it works in the lives of others. Sadly, Paul's letters are littered with the names of those who have succumbed to the subtlety of sin and the sickness of unbelief: Hymenaeus and Alexander, who veered from a good conscience and "made shipwreck of their faith" (1 Timothy 1:19–20); or Philetus, who "swerved from the truth" and spread corruption "like gangrene" (2 Timothy 2:17–18); or Demas, who deserted the faith because he was "in love with this present world" (2 Timothy 4:10).

Like the second and third seeds in Jesus' parable of the sower, these individuals professed faith but failed to keep fighting the fight of faith. For a season, they gave every appearance of being real, but the proof ultimately wasn't there. They didn't persevere.

Forsaking the faith doesn't happen instantly, but over time. Drifting usually begins discreetly, with illicit desire that turns into an overweening craving; and this craving, if unchecked, becomes compelling enough to lead you into temptation, entangle you in sin, and strip you of the desire to go on fighting the fight of faith. This is why Paul pleads with Timothy, like a father would plead with a son:

> But as for you, O man of God, flee these things. Pursue righteousness, godliness, faith, love, steadfastness, gentleness. *Fight the good fight of the faith.* Take hold of the eternal life to which you were called and about which you made the good confession in the presence of many witnesses.
>
> 1 Timothy 6:11–12, emphasis added

Fighting the good fight of the faith means we put on the whole armor of God. We need this if we're going to be strong in the Lord and succeed against the schemes of the devil (Ephesians 6:10–11). We need the shield of faith, with which we can extinguish the fiery darts of doubt that come from the evil one. But we also need to wield the sword of the Spirit, the Word of God (Ephesians 6:16–17). For there is no substitute for knowing God's Word and being able to draw upon its convicting truth.

When temptation arises, we need to have the Word of God close at hand, so we can stab sin in the belly and render it ineffective. Every time we feel discouraged or deflated or tempted to do something we shouldn't, we ought to stop and meet temptation head-on with the sword of the Spirit, the Word of God. Fight against the desire to sin by feeding upon the promises of Scripture. This is how Jesus continued in the faith (see Matthew 4:1–11). This is how we will continue in the faith.

FINISH THE RACE

Real Christians not only fight the fight of faith; they also finish the race. Regardless of the distance, they don't quit. Despite the terrain, they press forward. Although they're fatigued, they endure to the finish line. Completing their course is proof that they're real.

I admire those who run marathons. I've not run one, and frankly never plan to. Truth be told, I don't want to. Part of my problem is I can't imagine crossing the ten- or twenty-mile marker without stopping to congratulate myself on how far I've come! To run even a dozen miles would be a huge personal accomplishment—and I'd want crowds to cheer, someone to take my picture, and an official to hand me a big shiny trophy!

It's tempting to view the Christian life that way. It's easy to think that what counts is how we begin, or how far we go, or how long we run. But the only thing that ultimately counts is whether we cross the finish line and complete the race.

Paul was fixated on finishing his race: "Not that I have already obtained this or am already perfect, but *I press on* to make it my own, because Christ Jesus has made me his own" (Philippians 3:12, emphasis added). And he declares, "I do not account my life of any value nor as precious to myself, *if only I may finish my course* and the ministry that I received from the Lord Jesus, to testify to the gospel of the grace of God" (Acts 20:24, emphasis added).

Of course, if the Christian life were a gentle downward slope, we wouldn't need to stress running the race with perseverance. All we would need to do is find ourselves a comfy chair with well-greased wheels, sit down in it, give ourselves a little nudge, and coast across the finish line, kicked back and enjoying the ride.

But the race isn't downhill; it's uphill. And the way forward isn't easy, but hard. Jesus didn't hide this from us, but says plainly, "Enter by the narrow gate. For the gate is wide and the way is easy that leads to destruction, and those who enter by it are many. For the gate is narrow and the way is hard that leads to life, and those who find it are few" (Matthew 7:13–14).

Christian, the main character in John Bunyan's *Pilgrim's Progress*, is on his way to the Celestial City when he comes to the foot of a hill. There he sees the path forward, but it goes up the hill. He reads the sign; the path is called Difficult. But he also notices two other paths; they both go around the hill, one to the left and one to the right. He watches as some fellow travelers to the Celestial City take one of these routes around the hill.

But Christian notices the names of these alternative paths. The first route is called Danger, the second, Destruction. He sees they don't lead to the Celestial City, and at once realizes there's only one way to finish his course—to run the race uphill, along the path called Difficult.

So it is for every Christian. The race is hard, and the path goes uphill. This is why the book of Hebrews encourages us, "Therefore, since we are surrounded by so great a cloud of witnesses, let us also lay aside every weight, and sin which clings so closely, and let us *run with endurance* the race that is set before us, looking to Jesus, the founder and perfecter of our faith" (Hebrews 12:1–2, emphasis added).

If we're going to run with endurance, we must draw

strength from the great cloud of witnesses—the examples of those who have gone before us, who have completed their race, who have stayed faithful over a lifetime. We must also drop the deadweight we're carrying. If we're going to finish our race, we've got to throw off sin, which clings so closely; no one completes the Boston Marathon with a fifty-pound pack slung over his back. And we must keep our eyes fixed on Jesus, who has already finished his race and shown us the way. Like Christ, we must concentrate our gaze on the joy set before us so we can endure to the end, just as he did.

KEEP THE FAITH

Real Christians not only run perseveringly; they hold on to the faith tenaciously. They keep a tight grip on the truth of the gospel and don't let go. At the end of life, they say with Paul, "I have kept the faith" (2 Timothy 4:7). Keeping the faith is proof that we're real.

Real Christians realize there are real *threats* to the faith. That's why they don't shrug their shoulders when Scripture warns, "Your adversary the devil prowls around like a roaring lion, seeking someone to devour" (1 Peter 5:8), or when it reads, "even Satan disguises himself as an angel of light," and looks for someone to deceive (2 Corinthians 11:14), or when they hear, "It is the last hour, and as you have heard that antichrist is coming, so now many antichrists have come" (1 John 2:18).

So, too, real Christians take Jesus seriously when he says, "If you abide in my word, you are truly my disciples" (John 8:31). And they listen to Paul's charge to Timothy as a word to them: "Guard the deposit entrusted to you" (1 Timothy 6:20).

If we're going to keep the faith, we've got to grow in our understanding of the faith. This means we move past the doctrinal ABCs and "go on to maturity" (Hebrews 6:1), digesting solid food that increases our discernment (Hebrews 5:14) and attaining mature manhood so we're not "tossed to and fro by the waves and carried about by every wind of doctrine" (Ephesians 4:14).

To help believers grow in God's Word, the Lord gives the church pastors and elders who are responsible to shepherd God's flock by faithfully teaching God's Word. Paul's protégé, Timothy, had this role within the early church, which is why Paul exhorts him with such weighty words: "I charge you in the presence of God and of Christ Jesus, who is to judge the living and the dead, and by his appearing and his kingdom: preach the word; be ready in season and out of season; reprove, rebuke, and exhort, with complete patience and teaching" (2 Timothy 4:1–2).

ONCE SAVED, ALWAYS SAVED?

Because the Bible emphasizes perseverance, Christians sometimes mistakenly think this means they can't enjoy the assurance of salvation. If we have to persevere to the end, how can we be confident that once we are saved, we are always saved? Can we ever be sure of our salvation, if we have to go on fighting the fight of faith and never give up?

This is more than a theoretical question; it's an intensely practical one. Some of us have a son or daughter, a brother or sister, a college roommate or next-door neighbor, who once made a profession of faith yet now appears to want to have nothing to do with Jesus. These situations are heartbreaking, and they force us to ask tough questions.

I often hear Christians talk about the doctrine of eternal security as though it means once saved, always saved — *no matter what you do*. This is the idea that you can profess faith and "get saved" — and then live however you want without your life in any way calling into question your salvation. But the Bible won't let us get away with that. Scripture insists: once saved, always saved — *as seen by what you do*.[61]

Paul was confident of the eternal security of believers, and he encouraged them to have this same assurance. "I am sure of this," he says to the believers in Philippi, "that he who began a good work in you will bring it to completion at the day of Jesus Christ" (Philippians 1:6). Paul's confidence of their salvation was inextricably linked to what he saw of their faith. As he says, it was "your partnership in the gospel from the first day until now" (verse 5) that gave him confidence in their right standing with Jesus.

Paul *assured* the Philippians of their salvation because he *saw* their faith in action. They not only entered into partnership with Paul but stuck with him through the ups and downs of ministry. Because of this tangible evidence of their authenticity, Paul can confidently say they are real.

We find this same line of reasoning as Paul speaks to the believers in Thessalonica. "For we know, brothers loved by God, that he has chosen you," Paul confidently says to them (1 Thessalonians 1:4). But how can he be so sure? Because of what he saw in their lives: "Our gospel came to you not only in word, but also in power and in the Holy Spirit and with full conviction" (verse 5).

Anyone can have this full assurance right now. All they need to do is entrust themselves to Jesus Christ, rely on him by faith, and believe he is able to forgive their sins through his death and resurrection. "Believe in the Lord Jesus, and you will be saved," is the simple scriptural formula (Acts 16:31). If this describes the attitude of your heart, you can freely rest in all that the Bible promises to those who have faith.

On the other hand, if we are living in unbelief, we can't enjoy the assurance of faith. We find the Bible's promises of salvation given only to those who have faith. It's not biblically wise or justified, then, to assure someone of their salvation who isn't walking in faith.[62]

To be sure, even real Christians lapse in their faith. Abraham, the model of faith, had seasons of doubt, which led to some dubious decisions. In fact, as we read Abraham's story in Genesis, we see enough spiritual ups and downs to make us want to get off that roller coaster. *But even though Abraham doesn't live perfectly, he does live perseveringly.* He always returns to the Lord. So it is with real Christians.[63]

A GOOD DIAGNOSTIC QUESTION

To have confidence when it comes to our eternal security, we need to learn to diagnose ourselves and others by asking the right questions. We often ask the question, "Have you accepted Jesus as your personal Savior?" Or, "When did you get saved?" But a far better question to ask is this: "Are you relying on Christ right now to meet all of your needs?" Or, "How is Christ working in your life?" It's critical to ask ourselves, and to ask others, not where they've been, but where they are right now.

Regardless of how far we've run or how strong we feel, we need to stay humble. Don't get cocky or strut, and definitely don't presume to have this whole Christian thing in the bag. "Pride goes before destruction," Proverbs reminds us, "and a haughty spirit before a fall" (16:18). Arrogance is perilous— often the prelude to a face-plant. "Therefore let anyone who thinks that he stands take heed lest he fall" (1 Corinthians 10:12).

The believers in Rome presumed upon their good standing, so Paul had to cut them down to size with a stern warning:

> So do not become proud, but fear. For if God did not spare the natural branches, neither will he spare you. Note then the kindness and the severity of God: severity toward those who have fallen, but God's kindness to you, provided you continue in his kindness. Otherwise you too will be cut off.
>
> Romans 11:20–22

If we want to persevere, we must also treat the warnings of Scripture not as enemies, but as friends. Sometimes believers are nervous about the warning passages of the Bible, as though they can somehow undermine our confidence in finishing the race. The book of Hebrews is filled with sober warnings about the necessity of persevering and the peril of failing to do so. And yet these warnings aren't adversaries to our faith; rather, God uses them to encourage us in the fight of faith so we keep running and don't give up.[64]

YOUR PERSEVERANCE IS GOD'S PRESERVATION

Although perseverance is proof that we're real, the good news is that our continuing in the faith doesn't ultimately depend on us. Our security isn't found in us, nor are we called on to *prove ourselves* by persevering in the faith, as though the Christian life was a performance review designed to convince God we are worthy of his grace and love.

Yes, perseverance proves we're real. But, more importantly, it proves *God* is real. If we keep the faith, God is seen to be faithful. When we finish the race, God shows himself strong. Our perseverance vindicates God's sustaining grace.

Perseverance proves God has given you a new heart, causing you to walk in his ways and keep his statutes (see Ezekiel 36:26–27). Perseverance proves you have been born again: "For everyone who has been born of God overcomes the world" (1 John 5:4). And perseverance proves you have been given eyes to see, because now "with unveiled face, beholding the glory of the Lord, [you] are being transformed into the same image from one degree of glory to another" (2 Corinthians 3:18).

The best thing we can do to remain secure is to entrust ourselves to God each day. Charles Spurgeon is exactly right on this point: "If you trust yourselves to God, he will preserve you; but if you try to keep yourselves, you will fail."[65] This is the key to enjoying eternal security — *entrust yourself to God*. For he will *preserve* you and bring you safely to your heavenly home.

"He who calls you is faithful; he will surely do it" (1 Thessalonians 5:24).

CHAPTER RESOURCES

QUESTIONS FOR REFLECTION

1. Read the following passages: Mark 13:13; Acts 11:23; 13:43; 14:21 – 22; 2 Timothy 4:6 – 8; Revelation 2:2 – 3; 3:10 – 11. What does each passage have to say about persevering in the faith?

2. The apostle Paul said to new believers, "Through many tribulations we must enter the kingdom of God" (Acts 14:22). But we don't often hear Christians encouraging each other in this way. Why is that?

3. When we read the letters of Paul, he often seems fixated on the future, on finishing the race (see Acts 20:24; Philippians 3:12 – 14). Do you know people who have a fixation on the future and finishing the race well? What characterizes their lives?

4. Read Hebrews 12:1 – 2. To finish the race, we're called to lay aside every weight and the sin that clings so closely. What sin is slowing you down? What concrete steps can you take to lay it aside?

5. Hebrews 12:1 – 2 also calls us to fix our eyes on Jesus. In your breakout time, share how your group can encourage you to fix your eyes on Jesus.

6. Ask yourself this question: Am I presuming upon the grace of God, or am I today trusting in the person of Christ? Then share with a friend or spouse your answer to this question.

SCRIPTURES TO PONDER

- 1 Samuel
- Job
- 2 Timothy
- Hebrews
- 1 Peter

BOOKS TO HELP YOU DIG DEEPER

Berkouwer, G. C. *Faith and Perseverance*. Studies in Dogmatics. Grand Rapids: Eerdmans, 1973.

Fernando, Ajith. *The Call to Joy and Pain: Embracing Suffering in Your Ministry*. Wheaton, IL: Crossway, 2007.

Schreiner, Thomas R. *Run to Win the Prize: Perseverance in the New Testament*. Wheaton, IL: Crossway, 2010.

Biographies for Encouragement

Kuhn, Isobel. *Green Leaf in Drought*. 1957. Reprint, Littleton, CO: OMF International, 2007.

Piper, John. *The Roots of Endurance: Invincible Perseverance in the Lives of John Newton, Charles Simeon, and William Wilberforce*. Wheaton, IL: Crossway, 2002.

ten Boom, Corrie. *The Hiding Place*. 1971. Reprint, Peabody, MA: Hendrickson, 2009.

Wurmbrand, Richard. *Tortured for Christ*. 1968. Reprint, Bartlesville, OK: Living Sacrifice, 1998.

10

THIS MAGIC
CALLED REAL

As this book draws to an end, the time has come to ask yourself, *Am I real?* Jesus wasn't afraid to ask would-be followers this question. Do you remember how he probed Simon Peter, the one who three times denied knowing him: "Simon, son of John, do you love me?" (John 21:16). This was Jesus' way of asking Simon Peter, "Are you real?"

Or recall the challenge Paul put to the Christians in Corinth: "Examine yourselves, to see whether you are in the faith." He had a simple way of defining what it meant to be real: "Jesus Christ is in you" (2 Corinthians 13:5). Paul wants these believers to ponder whether they see the living Christ at work in their lives. Are they real?

It's not only biblical to ask yourself this question; it's also wise for one simple reason — *a day is coming when we will all have to get real.* We refer to that day as the day of judgment. The Bible calls it, appropriately so, a day of revelation, "when God's righteous judgment will be revealed" (Romans

2:5), when "God judges the secrets of men by Christ Jesus" (verse 16), when the Lord "will bring to light the things now hidden in darkness and will disclose the purposes of the heart" (1 Corinthians 4:5), and when appearances won't fool anyone—only realities of the heart will count (see Romans 2:25–29).

On that day, no one will be able to cover the nakedness of an unregenerate heart or an unchristian life with the fig leaf of a profession of faith. Everything will be laid bare before the eyes of him to whom we must give an account (see Hebrews 4:13). And yet, on that day, if you realize you're not real, it will be too late to get real. Your surprise at your own spiritual state will only serve as testimony to seal your fate.

We must get real *now*, because we will all have to get real later. And it is infinitely better to be surprised about the state of your soul now than to be caught off guard then. In this life you still have an opportunity to change. On that day, it will be too late.

THE VELVETEEN RABBIT GOT IT RIGHT

The Velveteen Rabbit is one of my favorite children's stories. It is the story of a toy rabbit that desperately wants to be a real rabbit. And the Velveteen Rabbit got it right. Throughout this book we've been asking the same question he asked his old friend, the Skin Horse:

> "What is REAL?" asked the Rabbit one day, when they were lying side by side near the nursery fender, before Nana came to tidy the room. "Does it mean having things that buzz inside you and a stick-out handle?"
>
> "Real isn't how you are made," said the Skin Horse. "It's a

thing that happens to you. When a child loves you for a long, long time, not just to play with, but REALLY loves you, then you become Real."

"Does it hurt?" asked the Rabbit.

"Sometimes," said the Skin Horse, for he was always truthful. "When you are Real, you don't mind being hurt"...

"I suppose *you* are Real?" said the Rabbit. And then he wished he had not said it, for he thought the Skin Horse might be sensitive. But the Skin Horse only smiled.

"The Boy's Uncle made me Real," he said. "That was a great many years ago; but once you are Real you can't become unreal again. It lasts for always."

The Rabbit sighed. He thought it would be a long time before this magic called Real happened to him. He longed to become Real, to know what it felt like; and yet the idea of growing shabby and losing his eyes and whiskers was rather sad. He wished that he could become it without these uncomfortable things happening to him.[66]

For some of you, reading this book has been an encouraging experience. You know you're real because you *see* you're real—not through anxious introspection, but Spirit-driven action. You bear the marks of real and therefore enjoy the "full assurance of faith" (Hebrews 10:22). To use the apostle Peter's language, you have confirmed your calling and election (see 2 Peter 1:10).

For others, reading this book has raised questions for you. You realize there's more to being real than simply wanting to be real, or thinking you're real, or saying you're real. As a result, you're frankly not sure whether you are a real Christian. In the past, you've felt like your faith was authentic and your love for God genuine, but the lack of evidence in your own life has brought you to a different place. What you once called faith now seems far less real than it did.

If you've been honest with yourself as you've read this book, you may be at a point of admitting you don't see the marks of real in your life right now. You're not hostile to the Christian faith. Quite the opposite, in fact. You have a high regard for the Bible and believe Jesus died for your sins. And yet for some reason those convictions have not translated into a transformed life.

Perhaps you know this, but you want to become real. Like the Velveteen Rabbit, you long for this "magic called Real" to happen to you. You want to know what it feels like to be real. But like the Velveteen Rabbit, you're scared of what might happen if you become real — you're worried about all those "uncomfortable things" that may happen to you.

The invitation for you is to embrace Jesus Christ by faith — not merely by a mental assent to a set of historical facts about Jesus, but with heartfelt reliance on his person and work. Cry out to Jesus, trust in his provision, turn away from sin, give yourself to him entirely. And you will find Jesus faithful — and real.

IT LASTS FOR ALWAYS!

We become real, as the Skin Horse knows, when we're loved for a long, long time. Scripture, in fact, says that God loves his children "from everlasting to everlasting" (Psalm 103:17). What real Christians realize is God has loved them for a very, very long time — indeed, from "before the foundation of the world" (Ephesians 1:4).

If you're real, you know you have been the apple of God's eye from all eternity past. He has had you on his heart for longer than you can imagine. He's been forever excited about calling you his own.

Real is what happens to us when God places his sovereign love on us, calls us to himself, makes us his very own. And the best news of all — once you're real you can't become unreal again.

As the Skin Horse says, *"It lasts for always!"*

ACKNOWLEDGMENTS

I'm delighted to acknowledge the many individuals who have had a hand in helping me bring this book together. Pride of place goes to my wife, Katie, who is a constant source of encouragement and joy. Nothing of value happens in my life without her having a major part in it!

Several friends read earlier drafts of the book and offered helpful feedback: Ben Wilson, Rae Wilson, Beth Jones, Andy Isch, John Isch, Ted Griffin, Randy Hess, Jeremy Mann, Joel Bain, and a top-notch group of Calvary interns! I'm grateful to all of them for giving their time and insight to strengthen the book in many ways. The whole team at Zondervan has been a delight to work with; I owe special thanks to my editor, Ryan Pazdur, whose enthusiasm and expertise helped shepherd this project along.

This book began life as a sermon series preached at Calvary Memorial Church, where I have the privilege of serving as pastor. The many conversations that ensued as a result of the series helped refine my thinking and thus improve the final shape of this book. To the elders, ministry staff, and congregation, I'm deeply indebted.

Finally, I'd like to dedicate this book to two of the most real Christians I know — Tom and Julie Steller. Katie and I had the privilege of doing life and ministry together with the Stellers for two years after college. Their self-forgetful and Jesus-pursuing way of life — always eager to see Christ get credit for everything — marked our lives indelibly. We'll always have the fondest affection for our time together at 1604 Elliot Avenue!

Soli Deo Gloria!

NOTES

1. Chris Welch and Gregory Wallace, "Santorum: Obama Leads with a 'Different Theology,'" CNN. com, http://politicalticker.blogs.cnn.com/2012/02/18/ santorum-obama-leads-with-a-different-theology/ (accessed March 3, 2014).
2. David Kinnaman and Gabe Lyons, *Unchristian: What a New Generation Really Thinks about Christianity... and Why It Matters* (Grand Rapids: Baker, 2007).
3. See David Fitch, *The End of Evangelicalism? Discerning a New Faithfulness for Mission: Towards an Evangelical Political Theology* (Eugene, OR: Wipf & Stock, 2011).
4. In his biography of Jonathan Edwards, Iain H. Murray notes, "Edwards never gave closer and more careful thought to anything than he did to this" (*Jonathan*

Edwards: A New Biography [Edinburgh: Banner of Truth, 1987], 252).

5. Jonathan Edwards, *The Works of Jonathan Edwards, vol. 2: Religious Affections*, ed. John E. Smith (1959; repr., New Haven, CT: Yale University Press, 2009).

6. For expositions of Jonathan Edwards's *Religious Affections*, see Gerald R. McDermott, *Seeing God: Jonathan Edwards and Spiritual Discernment* (Vancouver, B.C.: Regent, 2000), and C. Samuel Storms, *Signs of the Spirit: An Interpretation of Jonathan Edwards'* Religious Affections (Wheaton, IL: Crossway, 2007).

7. I owe this phrasing to a comment made by John E. Smith, editor of the Yale edition of *Religious Affections*: "Not only do they [the signs] serve as tests or standards of genuine piety, but they are themselves the very substance of the religious life" (p. 11).

8. See Collin Hansen, *Young, Restless, Reformed: A Journalist's Journey with the New Calvinists* (Wheaton, IL: Crossway, 2008).

9. See Matthew Lee Anderson, "Here Come the Radicals!" *Christianity Today*, March 15, 2013, www .christianitytoday.com/ct/2013/march/here-come-radicals.html (accessed March 3, 2014).

10. See Ross Douthat, *Bad Religion: How We Became a Nation of Heretics* (New York: Free Press, 2012).

11. Here I agree with Jonathan Edwards that when Scripture speaks of transformed character (or what he calls "Christian practice") as the best evidence of our being real, it presupposes that we believe the essentials of the Christian faith. In his own words, the profession of

Christianity "is not the main thing in the evidence, nor anything distinguishing in it; yet 'tis a thing requisite and necessary in it" (*Religious Affections*, 412).

12. C. S. Lewis, "Men without Chests," in *The Abolition of Man* (1944; repr., San Francisco: HarperSanFrancisco, 2001), 1–26.

13. See the famous essay by Princeton stalwart B. B. Warfield, "On the Emotional Life of Our Lord," in *Biblical and Theological Studies: A Commemoration of 100 Years of Princeton Seminary* (New York: Scribner's, 1912), 35–90.

14. I'm indebted to A. W. Tozer for the expressions "twice-born" and "once-born"; see his "The Once-Born and Twice-Born," in *The Best of A. W. Tozer: Book Two* (Camp Hill, PA: WingSpread, 2007), 159.

15. As Jonathan Edwards observes, "Indeed allowances must be made for the natural temper: conversion does not entirely root out the natural temper: those sins which a man by his natural constitution was most inclined to before his conversion, he may be most apt to fall into still." But Edwards balances this with an important caveat: "But yet conversion will make a great alteration *even with respect to these sins*" (*Religious Affections*, 341, emphasis added).

16. Quoted in Arnold Dallimore, *George Whitefield: The Life and Times of the Great Evangelist of the Eighteenth-Century Revival*, vol. 1 (1970; repr., Edinburgh: Banner of Truth, 1980), 73, emphasis added.

17. C. S. Lewis, *Mere Christianity* (1952; repr., New York: Macmillan, 1960), 114.

18. I should acknowledge that my understanding of humility is at some variance with Jonathan Edwards, who defines humility as "a sense that a Christian has of his own utter insufficiency, despicableness, and odiousness, with an answerable frame of heart" (*Religious Affections*, 311). That being said, Edwards is specifically referring to what he calls "evangelical humiliation," and contrasting it with "legal humiliation." When this distinction is taken into account, my view is closer to his (see *Religious Affections*, 311–12).

19. I owe the phrase "transcendent self-confidence" to a comment made by Robert C. Roberts in his masterful treatment of humility in his book, *Spiritual Emotions: A Psychology of Christian Virtues* (Grand Rapids: Eerdmans, 2007), 81.

20. Edwards, *Religious Affections*, 315.

21. Lewis, *Mere Christianity*, 114.

22. See Roger Steer, *Basic Christian: The Inside Story of John Stott* (Downers Grove, IL: InterVarsity, 2009), 271–72.

23. Lewis, *Mere Christianity*, 99.

24. See Robert V. Remini, *The Life of Andrew Jackson* (Newtown, CT: American Political Biography Press, 2003), 340–41.

25. I owe the phrase "a lamblike disposition" to Jonathan Edwards (*Religious Affections*, 356).

26. Edwards, *Religious Affections*, 345.

27. Jonathan Edwards, "Images of Divine Things," in *The Works of Jonathan Edwards, vol. 11: Typological Writings* (New Haven, CT: Yale University Press, 1993), 74.

28. Edwards, *Religious Affections*, 351.

29. Remini, *Life of Andrew Jackson*, 341.

30. Ibid.

31. In this chapter I am significantly indebted to Robert C. Roberts (*Spiritual Emotions*, 97–113), both for his understanding of humility and for his understanding of other emotions that look like, but aren't the same as, humility.

32. I owe this language to Roberts, *Spiritual Emotions*, 108–9.

33. See the classic study by Karl A. Menninger, *Whatever Became of Sin?* (New York: Hawthorn, 1973), or the more recent study by Cornelius Plantinga Jr., *Not the Way It's Supposed to Be: A Breviary of Sin* (Grand Rapids: Eerdmans, 1995).

34. Cited in David Wells, *The Courage to Be Protestant: Truth-lovers, Marketers, and Emergents in the Post-modern World* (Grand Rapids: Eerdmans, 2008), 102.

35. I owe this way of putting it to Jonathan Edwards (*Religious Affections*, 358).

36. See the magnificent sermon by Jonathan Edwards ("The Excellency of Christ," in *The Works of Jonathan Edwards, vol. 19: Sermons and Discourses 1734–1738*, ed. M. X. Lesser [New Haven, CT: Yale University Press, 2001], 560–96) in which he expounds on the "admirable conjunction of diverse excellencies in Jesus Christ" (p. 565).

37. Edwards, *Religious Affections*, 347.

38. Charles H. Spurgeon, *Lectures to My Students* (1875; repr., Peabody, MA: Hendrickson, 2010), 77–78.

39. Howard Taylor and Geraldine Taylor, *Hudson Taylor's Spiritual Secret* (Grand Rapids: Discovery House, 1990), 134–35.

40. Ibid., 136.

41. Quoted in Elisabeth Elliot, *Through Gates of Splendor* (1956; repr., Carol Stream, IL: Tyndale, 1996), 17.

42. A. W. Tozer, *The Pursuit of God* (Harrisburg, PA: Christian Publications, 1948), 16 (emphasis added).

43. See Edwards, *Religious Affections*, 383.

44. Jonathan Edwards, "Striving after Perfection," in *The Works of Jonathan Edwards, vol. 19: Sermons and Discourses 1734–1738*, ed. M. X. Lesser (New Haven, CT: Yale University Press, 2001), 688.

45. See John Piper, *When I Don't Desire God: How to Fight for Joy* (Wheaton, IL: Crossway, 2004).

46. Tozer, *Pursuit of God*, 16.

47. Ibid., 13.

48. This prayer is taken from the end of Tozer's first chapter in *Pursuit of God*, 20.

49. Quoted in Eric Metaxas, *Bonhoeffer: Pastor, Martyr, Prophet, Spy* (Nashville: Nelson, 2011), 321.

50. David P. Gushee, "Following Jesus to the Gallows," *Christianity Today*, April 3, 1995, 30.

51. Malcolm Muggeridge, *A Third Testament* (Boston: Little, Brown, & Co., 1976), 180.

52. Francis A. Schaeffer, *The Mark of the Christian* (Downers Grove, IL: InterVarsity, 1970), 15.

53. Martyn Lloyd-Jones, *The Love of God: Studies in 1 John* (Wheaton, IL: Crossway, 1994), 172.

54. Oswald Chambers, *My Utmost for His Highest* (1935;

repr., Uhrichsville, OH: Barbour, 2010), 146 (selection
for May 21).

55. See Timothy K. Beougher and Lyle W. Dorsett, eds.,
    Accounts of a Campus Revival: Wheaton College, 1995
    (1995; repr., Eugene, OR: Wipf & Stock, 2002).

56. D. Martyn Lloyd-Jones, *The Unsearchable Riches of
    Christ: An Exposition of Ephesians 3* (Grand Rapids:
    Baker, 1979), 253.

57. Cathy Lee Grossman, "Young Adults Aren't Sticking
    with the Church," *USA Today*, August 6, 2007, http://
    usatoday30.usatoday.com/news/religion/2007-08-06-
    church-dropouts_N.htm (accessed March 10, 2014).

58. See Mike McKinley, *Am I Really a Christian?* (Whea-
    ton, IL: Crossway, 2011), 77.

59. Charles Haddon Spurgeon, "Enduring to the End," in
    Spurgeon's Expository Encyclopedia, vol. 12 (1951; repr.,
    Grand Rapids: Baker, 1996), 293.

60. Ibid., 292.

61. I owe this way of expressing things to my friend and
    former teacher Scott Hafemann.

62. Jonathan Edwards has especially astute things to say
    about this (see *Religious Affections*, 175–81).

63. Edwards writes, "True saints may be guilty of some
    kinds and degrees of backsliding, and may be soiled by
    particular temptations, and may fall into sin, yea great
    sins: but they can never fall away so, as to grow weary
    of religion, and the service of God, and habitually to
    dislike it and neglect it; either on its own account, or
    on account of the difficulties that attend it" (*Religious
    Affections*, 390).

64. See Thomas R. Schreiner and Ardel B. Caneday, chapter 4, "Running to Win the Prize," in *The Race Set Before Us: A Biblical Theology of Perseverance and Assurance* (Downers Grove, IL: InterVarsity, 2001), 142–213.
65. Charles Haddon Spurgeon, "The Preservation of Christians in the World," in *Spurgeon's Expository Encyclopedia*, vol. 12 (1951; repr., Grand Rapids: Baker, 1996), 283.
66. Margery Williams, *The Velveteen Rabbit: Or How Toys Become Real* (New York: Macmillan, 1983), 4–6.